La Pomme de Portland

a collection of stories & recipes drawn from the seasons of food & life

Written and Photographed
by
Carrie Minns

ALLISON
Happy Mother's Day!
all my best,
Carrie Minns

Fern & Flora, Co.

First Edition
ISBN 978-1-7320836-0-8
Copyright © 2018
Fern & Flora, Co.
www.fernandfloraco.com

Written, photographed, and taste tested in Portland, OR
Printed in the United States of America

Disclaimer: Although each recipe was tested multiple times and a handful of us painstakingly combed through each one to ensure 100% accuracy, mistakes are part of our human nature, especially for those of us battling presbyopia. Should you come across a mistake in a recipe, please accept my deepest apologies and don't hesitate to get ahold of me through my website for the correction. Cheers!

The La Pomme de Portland Team
Carrie Minns – Chief Wordsmith, Photographer, and Recipe Developer
www.carrieminns.com
Courtney Cook – Chief Graphic Designer and Book Layout Wonder Woman
www.courtneyffd.com
Meg DesCamp – Chief Editor/Copy Editor and Queen of the Details, Details, Details
www.megdescamp.com

For Dave, Hanna, Jack, and Will
Thank you for letting me share through words, photos, and food the time when we
all lived together in a house by the woods with a cat and a dog.

In memory of my mom, Betty Jane Rice Cook,
who is missed every minute of every day.

CONTENTS

A NOTE TO YOU FROM ME

Back when my hubby and I were first married, we were invited to a family dinner at my Granny's house. My Granny was a tall Norwegian woman named Esther who didn't hug much and signed all of her cards, *Fondly, Granny*. When answering machines entered our lives, her messages were simply, "Call, Granny." She canned kimchi every year wearing rubber gloves and made pink applesauce tinted by red-hot candies. She pruned bonsai, oil-painted chickadees in cherry trees, and had nasty cats that she fed tuna, bacon, and asparagus. She drank Old Fashioneds and smoked unfiltered cigarettes that she would rap on a hard surface before lighting up.

We never wanted to be caught trying to filch the grape or orange soda pop she had in her pantry because she'd come after us with a broom. For family gatherings, she ordered out for fried chicken or a honey ham and she served pies from her favorite restaurant. She often advised, "If you gain five pounds, lose it, because five becomes ten and ten becomes twenty, and pretty soon you've let yourself go." She created magical Christmas seasons for us complete with Christmas mice, eggnog sprinkled with nutmeg, and $100 checks in our stockings.

She also had the look — a no-nonsense, austere look that could stop even the most determined child from sneaking candy out of her "surprise drawer."

At our family dinner with my hubby, we had finished our meal of fried chicken and mashed potatoes and were sitting around in her living room talking. At some point, my hubby put his arm around my shoulders, then reached up and twirled some of my hair with his fingers — probably more out of nervousness than tenderness. This twirling caught my Granny's eye. She leaned forward out of her chair and said to the entire room, "What is *he* doing? Is he *playing* with her *hair?*"

She stared us down with the *look* then slowly leaned back in her chair with a "Hmmph!" and an upturn of the chin. Instantly, my hubby took his arm off my shoulders.

Even though my Granny passed away quite long ago, this story has been told over and over at almost every family gathering since it happened and we still laugh about it. Telling the story keeps my Granny alive to all of us and connects those of us who knew her, because whether we were there when the story took place or not, we can all picture exactly what happened. We can chuckle about her funny standoffishness and be grateful for her love of family gatherings and of Christmas.

We all cherish our independence and like to think we can handle life on our own, however, we humans are social creatures. We draw comfort from one another, from knowing that we're all experiencing some of the same successes or the same challenges, from knowing that we're not alone in these messy yet beautiful lives we live. We connect with one another in these ways by sharing stories. The details of my stories may be different from yours but often the sentiment is the same — love, loss, regret, celebration.

Most of the time, food is the catalyst that brings us together — parents, children, grandparents, sisters, brothers, friends — to share our stories. Food is a kind of bridge to our humanity. I started insisting on dinners together when my children were little. Nothing fancy. No complicated food or perfect table manners. Just that we meet at the dinner table to nourish ourselves and share stories from our day. In those early years, our dinner was often ended by my husband declaring he was about to have a heart attack because it was impossible to enjoy his food while our littlest one, Will, kept jumping up out of his chair, our middle one, Jack, kept telling wisecracks at the table, and our eldest, Hanna, kept leaning so far back in her chair that she tipped over…again and again. But I persevered.

Now, I believe my kids as well as my husband look forward to dinnertime. Yes, I still have to remind Will to sit in his chair, the teenagers to turn off their mobile phones, and my hubby to turn off the TV, and due to everyone's busy schedule, these family dinners don't happen every night. But when they do, I know we're grateful for the time together. We look forward to hearing stories about a funny teacher, a goofy friend, difficult customers, or how the dog spent his day. We get a glimpse into each other's day that we otherwise wouldn't have.

This book is like pulling up a chair to my kitchen table. This is the food I feed to my family and friends. These are the stories I tell them. When I want to make ragù for my family, I make the ragù in this book. When I want to make them chocolate chip cookies, I make the chocolate chip cookies in this book. We don't need a lot of complicated recipes in our cooking repertoire. It's okay to make the same dishes over and over (hence the tradition of Taco Tuesday at our house). There are reasons that recipes get handed down: because they are tried and true, because they are loved, because the familiar is comforting, and because they tie us to the person who originally made them for us.

I hope that you'll make my recipes, and in doing so, you'll be inspired to put your own spin on them, to write your changes in the margins, and to turn them into your own beloved dishes for your family and friends.

We have so much uncertainty in our world. One of the greatest gifts we can give others is to nourish and comfort them through food and stories. I hope that holding this book in your hands will be a tangible and gentle reminder to gather those you love around your kitchen table.

Fondly,

Carrie

A FEW WORDS TO READ **BEFORE** YOU MAKE THE RECIPES

My love for feeding those I care about started *not* in the kitchen but in the garden. My mother was a living encyclopedia of all things flowers, trees, and shrubs. She regularly decorated our kitchen table with vases full of cuttings from whichever flowers were blooming in our yard that day. A sunny day spent weeding and deadheading was my mom's idea of a perfect day. My grandfather (who was married to Granny and always called her "Mother") specialized in growing strawberries, apples, and orchids on his four acres in Milwaukie, Oregon and my dad (Granny's son who also called her "Mother") has always had a backyard vegetable garden.

The grandest and most memorable vegetable garden my dad ever tended was the one he planted in the front yard of my childhood home on Whidbey Island, Washington. Each spring, he pulled my brother, sister, and me in the trailer behind his tractor to a nearby farm where we'd pick up a load of manure. He'd then seat us around the pile of dung and haul us back home where he'd dig that manure into the dirt before sowing his seeds. In late spring, he taught us to eat snow peas off the vine. In the summer, we plucked sweet cherry tomatoes and ate them with just as much fervor as we did chocolate Space Food Sticks. Come fall, my dad showed us how to dig potatoes up out of the warm soil like they were hidden Easter eggs. And in late fall, when the harvest was over, we watched as he rototilled the garden back into the earth, topped it with compost, and let it sit for the winter.

By watching and helping my parents and grandparents tend to their flowers, their fruits, and their vegetables, I came to understand that there was a natural rhythm to it all. Each plant had its season.

Recipes Organized by Season

When I'm trying to decide what to feed my family, I first ask myself, "Which fruits, vegetables, meats, or seafood are in season now?" The answer guides me in the meals I make for that specific week. This is why the recipes in this book are organized by season. Go to my website (www.carrieminns.com) to find a list of produce, meats, and seafood that are commonly at the peak of their harvest during each season. The lines between the seasons are not hard and fast. However, once you start training yourself and your friends and family to eat by season, you won't eat those tasteless, watery strawberries shipped to your grocery store in winter from the other end of the world, but you will patiently wait until you can eat locally grown luscious sweet strawberries ripened under your early summer sun.

A Bit About the Recipes

I implore you to please read each recipe all the way through before you make it. Some of them require resting periods or overnight soaking and such. I'd feel awful if you planned to make a meal from the book for your family but halfway through you realized you didn't have enough time. So please, don't skip this part. I'll know if you did. I have eyes in the back of my head. Or, at least, my granny always said she did and you don't want to mess with Granny.

Because I have a kiddo with food sensitivities, I don't use a lot of dairy in my recipes and the nuts in my recipes can easily be omitted. I like the focus of most of my recipes to be the produce. I also do not use a lot of salt in my recipes, but always have it on the table so people can add more if they would like.

You won't find many recipes for fanciful desserts in here. I simply don't make them very often. I never feel that well physically after I've eaten them, so most of the time it's not worth it to me. My sweets tend to be more rustic: traditional cookies and fruit pies. If I had my wedding to do over, I would serve chocolate chip cookies and pumpkin pies with vanilla ice cream on the side instead of wedding cake.

A Bit About the Ingredients

I believe delicious food is not about gourmet techniques or recipe lists with exotic ingredients. I believe it's about using food that's in season as well as using the highest quality ingredients you can find and afford. This does not mean the ingredients have to be expensive. Yes, you can buy imported butter from Ireland or France that's spectacular, but often you can find less expensive sweet cream butter churned locally that measures up just as well. Buying produce in season can also help lessen the pressure on your pocket book. Here in the Pacific Northwest—what I like to call the Apple Capital of the United States—I've noticed that the price for Honeycrisp apples differs up to $4.00 per pound between in season and out of season apples.

To preserve freshness, I keep all of my flours, nuts, and bread in the freezer except those that I am using within the current week. I keep all of my specialty oils in the refrigerator—sesame, walnut, grapeseed—to keep them from going rancid too quickly. I don't store my olive oil in the fridge but keep it in a cool dark place. Since I use it so often, it doesn't have a chance to go bad.

One final note about ingredients: you'll notice that I tend to favor thyme and rosemary in my recipes. This is because those herbs grow year round in my yard. I encourage you to plant both of them. They are hardy Mediterranean little buggers and bonus, deer aren't fond of rosemary, so I plant mine near my roses to deter those big-eyed, blossom-munching mammals from eating the buds. I tell myself that it's helping.

A Bit About Baking

Baking is a fairly unforgiving little task; as in chemistry, all elements must be just so for the experiment to work well. I find it rather taxing on my brain, which is why I prefer to cook (much more forgiving), preferably with a glass of wine or a cup of tea in hand. However, when I take the time to bake and do it correctly, I'm usually quite pleased with the results and with myself.

First of all, when I bake I don't mess around with the ingredients. I usually use local unsalted butter, flour from a nearby mill, coarse Kosher salt, fresh eggs, the highest quality baking chocolate I can afford, and so on.

Many expert bakers insist on weighing out the proper amount of flour for a recipe because different flours have different weights based on how they're made and packaged, which can have an adverse affect on your baked goods. I have not gone to this extent, however, I do use the *dip and sweep* method to measure out my flour. What this means is that I take a big serving spoon and fluff up my flour in the bag. I then spoon it into my measuring cup and level the flour off with the back of a butter knife. This method always seems to garner good results for me.

While we're on the subject of baking, let's talk pie crust/pastry dough. I realize that there are a lot of perfectionists out there who insist that specific methods and equipment must be used in the making of pie crust: every single ingredient kept cold, butter cut in until it's exactly pea sized, marble counter top and marble rolling pin, and only a spec of dust used when rolling out your dough. Here's the thing, though. Most of us make this pastry dough for our family and/or our friends. We don't need five-star restaurant quality dough. I have a friend who makes huckleberry pies in the heat of summer. She rolls her dough out on an old linoleum tabletop using an empty wine bottle, and bakes her pies in a 9x11-inch glass baking dish. Her pies are devoured in minutes.

I myself usually roll out my dough on a pastry cloth that I inherited from my grandmother using a rolling pin with a cloth cover that looks like a ridged sock. If I'm feeling too lazy to set up the pastry cloth, then I simply sprinkle a little flour on my non-marble counter tops and roll my dough out there.

On the topic of keeping everything cold, yes, pastry dough does like to be cold, especially dough made with all butter. The trick is to keep the butter in its solid form as long as possible so that the flour and sugar have time to set up a bit in the oven before the butter melts; that way once the butter does melt, it will leave little air pockets behind, which is what leads to the coveted flaky crust. My challenge with pastry dough is not the making of the dough but the fact that I'm constantly interrupted—dog, kids, dog, kids, dog—and inevitably my dough sits out longer than it should. What I often do once I have my dough in the pie plate or laid out on a baking sheet is to pop it into the fridge while I'm making the filling. When I'm ready, I pull it out of the fridge, top it with the filling, and put it straight into my preheated oven.

One final note about pastry dough. I encourage you to always double your recipe. Use one half for whatever recipe you are currently making and pop the other half in the freezer where it keeps beautifully for up to three months. You never know when you might have a hankering to make a pie. For instance, maybe you have a significant other like mine who is so ecstatic at the start of blueberry season that he's been known to bring home three or four flats of warm, just-picked berries. I'm left with the job of using up those berries before they go bad, and of course blueberry hand pies are always on the list.

A Few Tips and Timesaving Techniques

I'm guessing most of you reading this book do not cook full time in a commercial kitchen with a sous chef and no distractions. You are doing your best to juggle multiple tasks a day, one of which is feeding your family in a kitchen with paper piles everywhere and a dishwasher that needs to be unloaded. Or is that just me? Below are a few of my tips for lightening the load ever so slightly.

I always use a timer; not because I can't cook by sight but because I'm constantly being interrupted. How many of us actually have the luxury of standing in front of a grill for 10-15 minutes straight, occasionally pressing on our meat as it cooks, and pulling it off at just the right instant? No, we're putting that meat on the grill and running back inside to chop up lettuce for a salad, dump pasta in a boiling pot of water, help the ten-year-old with math, and proofread the fifteen-year-old's essay that's due the next day and we completely forget about the meat on the grill…until the timer goes off reminding us to flip it. See? Use a timer. There's no shame in it.

When I make soups and most of my sauces, I don't cut everything up and then begin to sauté. Depending on the recipe, my routine looks something like this: While my pot is heating, I peel and dice half an onion. I add olive oil to the pot and while that's heating up, I dice the other half. I add the diced onions to the olive oil, give it all a stir, then I start peeling and dicing carrots, then celery, then dump it all in the pot with the onions. At that point I set the timer for eight minutes. While those veggies are softening, I mince garlic and chop up kale/spinach/sausages/whatever else needs chopping. Essentially, I use the cooking time to get the chopping done.

I mentioned up above to always double the recipe when making pastry dough. I also suggest you do this when you are making things like ragù, taco filling, favorite soup recipes, or even grilled meats. You will have leftovers and these leftovers are fabulous to stick in the freezer for a future dinner. Or, more often than freezing, I mix leftovers with brown rice, heat them up in the microwave, and slap them in a thermos for school lunches. Leftovers are also a fantastic afterschool snack for ravenous kiddos in the midst of puberty who claim, "There's nothing to eat in this house."

Those are just a few of my tips and techniques. I'm sure you have your own that you will incorporate when you make the recipes that fill these pages. If you have any questions, please don't hesitate to get hold of me through my website, www.carrieminns.com.

ENJOY!

Spring

AT THE BEGINNING…
HOMEMADE STRAWBERRY PRESERVES

A half-flat box of fragile strawberries balances against my protruding stomach. My right hand grips the outside of the box trying to anchor the precious load against myself. My other hand, my free hand, is not really free at all. It is weighed down with other purchases — a pound of slender French green beans, shiitake mushrooms I plan to sauté up later with a bit of butter and a sprinkling of sea salt, a bulbous spring onion that will probably find its way into a soup, and a dozen rhubarb macaroons for the kids, of course.

The smell from the flat is heady, intoxicating. Steadying myself, I glance around. A second's worth of panic ripples through my body until I have laid eyes on each child. Okay, they are here. They did not mistakenly follow another mother out of the crowd. Without a third hand to hold a child's, I call out, "Careful. Watch for cars. Stay by Mommy. Can one of you hold his hand?" The farther we get from the farmers market, the more the throngs dissipate. I can relax a bit, the excitement of my purchase growing.

While some couples choose to spend their alone time hitting flea markets or independent film releases, my hubby and I go to farmers markets and grocery stores. Instead of Sunday drives, we drag our children around to see food. Smell food. Taste food. When we hit the road, whether here or abroad, the first place we visit is the local grocery store or an outdoor market. We can't wait to see what they have to offer in that corner of the world. The dazzling colors and cornucopia of scents puts us on a high like a preschooler eating cotton candy.

Safely to the car, I herd the children into their seats. I take one last glance at the purchases I've laid in the back, hoping they won't spill during the ride. I drive off slow and steady. The warm, sweet smell immediately fills the whole car, silencing everyone in a sort of reverence as we make our way home.

I have had it in my head for quite some time this idea that we're on the cusp of a food revolution. Revolution is quite a loaded word — maybe it should be referred to as a food epiphany. A food revelation. A food manifesto, perhaps. I believe that everyone, at some level, realizes that our current relationship with food is toxic. Unhealthy. Just plain bad. But I can feel it. Smell it, even. The tide is turning and I find it fascinating. Thrilling even, to be here rediscovering what brought us together in the first place. Us and food. Back to the beginning of our relationship when it wasn't so cluttered

with words such as hormones, GMOs, and antioxidants. When it was simply, "Pick. Eat. Enjoy."

Some celebrate the first day of yachting season, baseball season, the holiday season...my hubby texts me photos to announce the opening of Hood season. Hood as in Hood strawberries. Those tiny little bundles of flavor whose June harvesting season is ever so fleeting. Those luscious, finger-staining berries grown only around the arch of the Willamette Valley and the Columbia Gorge. For three or four weeks, we buy them by the flat and promptly devour them. Every year we say we're going to buy extras and freeze them or can them to enjoy a little of summer in the depths of winter but that rarely happens.

I pull into the driveway. The children hop out and scatter. Anxiously walking around to the back, I flip open the trunk and pull out the undisturbed berries. I holler out to my hubby, "We're home!" I carefully place the load on the kitchen counter. My arms are weary but the Hood strawberries are safe. With nary a reference to maltodextrin or calories or any number of omegas, we stand around the flat, pluck off the little green caps, pop the berries into our mouths and swoon. So simple. So uncluttered. And again, I can feel it. The tide. It's turning.

HOMEMADE STRAWBERRY PRESERVES

Okay, people, you must read the directions all the way through. No skimming. Take note that this is a two-day, low sugar process. I like to use lemon juice and zest in my preserves, which are full of natural pectin, instead of store-bought pectin. If you double this recipe, you must separate the berry mixture into two pots to cook, otherwise your mixture will likely boil over, take 40 minutes to cook, and burn on the bottom. I may or may not know that from personal experience. And yes, canning strawberry preserves does take effort and concentration, but oh, how they will lift your spirits when you taste a bit of spring in the dead of winter.

4 pints freshly picked and hulled strawberries

Juice and zest from 1 lemon, juice strained for seeds, zest minced

1 1/2 cups sugar

Combine your strawberries and sugar in a large bowl. Press down on them with a potato masher, crushing some and leaving some whole. Cover and place your berries in the refrigerator overnight to macerate with the sugar.

When ready to can, lay out all of your supplies. Next, sterilize your jars in a canning pot filled with water to an inch above the jars. Bring to a boil and boil for 10 minutes. Turn down heat to low but leave your jars in there to stay hot. Place your lids in a small water-filled saucepan and simmer for 10 minutes. The rings do not need to be sterilized; just have them handy.

Add your lemon juice and zest to your berries and stir gently to combine.

Pour the berry mixture into a wide, heavy-bottomed pot. The level of the berry mixture should not be higher than halfway up. Bring the mixture to a rolling boil, stirring regularly so the bottom doesn't burn. As they cook, the preserves will darken and take on a shiny, candy-like sheen (similar to turning sugar into caramel). Continue to boil, 10 to 20 minutes, until the preserves reach 220°F, or they pass the plate test (after 10 minutes place a small spoonful of the berry liquid on a frozen saucer and put back in the freezer for 1 minute. If it stays in place when you run a finger through it and does not run back together, the preserves are done). Do the plate test at 15 minutes and at 20 minutes, if needed. Occasionally, skim the accumulating foam off the top. Once done, remove from heat.

Using your jar lifter, remove the sterilized jars from the canning pot, carefully pouring the water in each one back into the pot. Set them on your towels. Using a wide-mouth funnel, ladle the hot preserves into the jars, leaving ¼ inch of headspace.

Run a plastic knife along the inside edges of the jar to remove air bubbles. Wipe any stray jam off the jar with your damp towel. Using the magnetic lid lifter, place a lid on each jar. Screw on metal band just until tight.

Carefully, lower your filled jars back into the water bath. Bring to a boil and with the lid on, boil hard for 5 minutes. Remove from the water, and place on a towel out of the way to rest undisturbed for 24 hours. After one hour, you will start to hear a "ping" coming from the lids indicating they have sealed properly. After 24 hours, check to see if all of the lids have sealed by pressing down on the center of each one. If you can push down and make a popping sound, they haven't sealed. Stick any unsealed jars in the refrigerator and enjoy them over the next 2 to 3 weeks. The others can be stored in a cool, dark, dry place for up to a year. Enjoy.

YIELD: About 4 half pint jars

SUPPLIES FOR CANNING
4 half pint jars, 4 new lids, 4 rings, a large canning pot, a wide heavy-bottomed pot, a small saucepan, a candy thermometer, towels to place your jars on, a jar lifter, a ladle, a wide-mouth funnel, a ruler, a plastic knife, a magnetic lid lifter, a clean damp towel, and 3 small saucers put into the freezer

POTATO AND LEEK
BIRTHDAY SOUP

What is it about certain ages that stir our emotions? Emotions that are jubilant at one end and sometimes bittersweet at the other. You know the ages…1, 5, 13, 18, 40, 100 (if we should be so lucky).

My youngest just turned five and I'm feeling a bit melancholy about it. I don't know why. Maybe because he is the youngest and I know these stages don't last forever. He still brings me treasures like his older brother used to. Tiny daisies, crumpled dandelions, little rocks and sticks, all of which I slip into my pockets for safekeeping. I tell him that I put them in there to keep the treasures safe and any time I'm missing him, I pull one out. He's at that wonderful age where a flick of his hand lets you know how old he is. If he were with you right now he'd tell you that he's five, he has two loose teeth, and he starts kindergarten in the fall.

One of my dearest friends called recently. She had been looking at a photograph of the two of us with our eldest daughters. She said, "I look at that picture and they look so much older than I realized. I can't believe it."

Our daughters have grown up together since they were babies. I have loved watching them do just that, but looking at the photograph, I have to admit they are closer to the women they will become than the little girls they once were.

My daughter will be 13 in a month. I remember my 13th birthday well. Who was there. What I was wearing (purple velour). I received a tube of fruit-flavored lip gloss and my very own flute. How surreal that my daughter is an age I remember so vividly. And I wonder, if one of my children is that age…what does that make me?

My parents, my sister, my nephews, and the five of us were together last night to celebrate Will's fifth birthday. The grown-ups were around the dining room table. The kids were at the kitchen table. While we chatted, enjoyed our spring soup and sipped glasses of Pinot Gris, the boys tried their best to stay seated and eat, but more often than not, they were up. Banging out their compositions on the piano. Screeching by in their plastic cars. Asking for more applesauce, more bread, more cold water. We tried our best to ignore the chaos but it was proving difficult. I had almost reached my limit and was about to holler, "Enough!" but then I saw the look on my five-year-old's face. A look of pure joy. That all was as it should be. That the noise and the chaos were part of the celebration. And the fact that his cousins, his aunt, his nana and papa were all in town just for him was reason enough to scream from the top of his lungs. How could I put an end to the fanfare? This is what it feels like to be five. And before long, he'll know what it feels like to turn 13, just like his sister.

POTATO AND LEEK SOUP
WITH PETITE PEAS

Every year at this time I see recipes for Potato Leek Soup and every year I'm intrigued to make it. However, I'm not one to eat a pot full of warm milk, which is essentially how most of those soups are made. So, taking a cue from what was available at our local farmers market, I came up with this lighter version. I prefer the delicate balance of all the spring flavors in here just as it is but you could add a cup or so of shredded chicken, maybe from a leftover rotisserie chicken, to give it more heartiness. I would also have salt and pepper on the table so each person can give their soup a little zing right before eating. Believe it or not, this soup is delicious with soft- (or hard-) boiled eggs and some toast on the side. I have to admit that while I did serve this for my little guy's family birthday dinner, it was definitely more of a hit with the females in the group.

2 tablespoons olive oil

2 leeks diced, white and light green parts only, about 2 cups

1 teaspoon kosher salt

1/8 teaspoon freshly ground black pepper, or to taste

3 cloves garlic, peeled and thinly sliced

6 small Yukon gold potatoes diced (4 cups or so)

1/2 cup white wine

1 quart water or chicken broth or a combination of the two

1 cup fresh or frozen petite peas

A handful of minced fresh chives

Optional: 2 cups cooked, shredded chicken

In a large soup pot, heat your olive oil over medium heat. Add your leeks and salt to the pot. Sauté over med–low heat for about 5 minutes until leeks are softened. Stir occasionally so leeks do not burn. Add your garlic and sauté another minute or so. Stir in your wine and let the alcohol evaporate from the pot, about 2 to 3 minutes. I can always tell by sniffing the rising steam. Once the pungent alcohol smell turns sweet, you know it's finished. Now, add your potatoes (and chicken if you're using) and a quart of water/chicken broth plus enough water to cover the potatoes (and chicken if using) by about an inch. Bring to a boil, then turn the heat down and simmer for about 10 minutes. Add your peas and simmer another 5 minutes or until the potatoes are soft and the peas are just cooked. Spoon into shallow bowls and sprinkle with chives. Enjoy.

YIELD: Enough to serve a family of 4 plus one baby bird eater

STRAWBERRIES TO STIMULATE SUMMER

Well, think of it this way... at least the kids don't have spring fever. They're still willing to go to school," says my friend Jayne. She has a point. The kids don't have spring fever because we haven't had a spring. At this point, I believe we've surpassed the famous 40 days and 40 nights. Here we are at the beginning of June, and yesterday I woke up to the sound of my paper birch trees beating against the side of my house and fog as thick as the steam that rises from a boiling-over pasta pot.

I hang up the phone and tell myself no more whining. Never mind that I haven't planted my vegetable garden yet. Too soggy. Never mind that I actually had to use an umbrella yesterday. Unheard of by northwest natives. Never mind that my grass is at least six inches tall because I haven't been able to mow it due to the fact that it is currently a pool party for banana slugs. I don't even know if my push mower works on grass that tall. And yet if the weather isn't telling it, the fact that strawberries, blueberries, and cantaloupe are showing up in the markets tells me that somewhere…the sun is shining.

Embracing that thought, I take my butter out of the fridge, my flour and vanilla out of the pantry, and go to work creating the quintessential summer dessert: a strawberry tart. At five o'clock, I change out of my daily uniform of black athletic wear and red baseball hat and take the time to run a brush through my hair. I slap on my black wrap dress, pull on some boots — no amount of positive thinking can overcome the fact that the weather is definitely not indicative of strappy sandals — kiss my sweetie good-bye, and head off for an evening with the girls.

And sometimes, that's all we need, isn't it? A change of thoughts. A chance to mingle with the girls. Good conversation. Some delectable finger food. And a round of desserts: decadent chocolate soufflés, blackberry cheesecake, and a strawberry tart, all topped off with a flute of champagne. I drive home feeling quite effervescent. (And no, it isn't from the bubbles.)

This morning when I wake up the sun is out. She's gone now but she was there, if only for a few minutes. And her appearance, although ever so brief, helped.

TARTE AUX FRAISES

This is NOT a 30 minute dessert. You MUST READ all of the directions before you start. I'll know if you don't. You also need to have your egg yolks separated out before you begin. This is going to take time. I usually make my dough and pastry cream a day in advance. Will you have flour all over your counter and kitchen floor? Yes. Will there be dirty bowls and egg shells piled in the sink? Yes. Will your guests, your kids, your lover boy appreciate the time and effort it took to make this masterpiece? Maybe. Maybe not. But does it matter? You'll know what was behind this edible gift. Carry on, my friend. Carry on.

FOR THE PÂTE SUCRÉE
(Pastry Dough for Two 10-inch Tarts)

2 1/4 cups all-purpose flour

2/3 cup powdered sugar

1 teaspoon kosher salt

1 cup chilled unsalted butter, diced

1 egg yolk, room temperature

3 tablespoons milk

FOR THE CRÈME PÂTISSIÈRE
(Pastry Cream)

2 cups milk

1/2 cup sugar, divided

2 tablespoons all-purpose flour

2 tablespoons cornstarch

4 egg yolks, room temperature

2 teaspoons vanilla

2-3 cups fresh strawberries, washed, dried, and thickly sliced lengthwise

Optional: mint leaves for garnish

In a large bowl, or bowl of food processor, whisk/pulse together your flour, sugar, and salt. Cut in or pulse in your butter pieces until the dough resembles cornmeal, with a few pea-sized pieces of butter. Add in your egg yolk plus your milk, one tablespoon at a time, until the dough starts to come together. The dough should be soft and pliable, but not sticky.

Pour the whole concoction out onto a lightly floured surface and divide in half. Dust the top of one half with a bit of flour to prevent your hands from sticking to it. Channel your inner preschooler and press the dough into your tart pan. Push and press it around until it evenly covers the bottom and is at least halfway up the sides. Dust with more flour as necessary. Use a fork to prick some holes on the bottom. Cover and refrigerate for at least an hour or up to two days. Can also be frozen for a few months. Save the second half of your dough for a tart later in spring. A peach/blackberry tart, perhaps?

(Alternatively, you can shape your dough into two disks. Refrigerate for an hour or up to two days. Then roll out on a lightly floured surface and place in tart pan; this dough is quite stubborn to work with, so I find it easiest to avoid the rolling out part.)

When ready to bake your crust, preheat oven to 400°F. Take the dough out of the fridge, pop it in the oven, turn the heat down to 375°F, and bake for 15 to 18 minutes or until golden. Remove from oven and cool completely on a wire rack.

While your dough is chilling and/or baking, move on to your pastry cream. In a saucepan, heat your milk and ¼ cup of sugar over medium heat until it starts to bubble along the edges. Whisk occasionally to prevent burning.

While your milk is heating, whisk together your dry ingredients: ¼ cup sugar, flour, and cornstarch. Add your egg yolks and whisk together to make a yellow paste.

When milk is ready, slowly pour a bit of milk into the egg paste, whisking constantly. Do NOT pour your eggs into the hot milk or they will scramble. Continue to whisk and slowly pour the milk into the egg mixture. Once the two have been fully incorporated, pour the entire concoction back into the saucepan. Continue whisking over medium heat for 2 minutes. The cream will start to thicken and resemble vanilla pudding. Do not fret if you end up with a few small scrambled bits in your cream. You can always strain those out with a fine sieve. This isn't a five star restaurant, for heaven's sake.

Once the cream has thickened, remove from heat. Mix in your vanilla extract. Pour the fragrant cream into a decent-sized bowl. Take a large piece of plastic wrap and press it down on top of the cream. By doing this, you are trying to prevent the air from reaching the top and forming a skin. Toss your crème in the fridge to cool completely.

To assemble your Tarte aux Fraises (fancy French for strawberry tart), evenly spread a generous amount of your cooled cream into your prepared tart crust. (Eat the leftovers at midnight with a spoon.) Take your strawberry slices and make a spiral design on top. Garnish with a few mint leaves here and there, if you'd like. Set your masterpiece on a cake stand and let people ooh and ahh over it for a bit. Before they start double-dipping their fingers into the cream, cut into pizza slices and serve. Enjoy!

PS: Yes, I know that most fruit tarts are finished off with a jelly glaze. Not mine. I have a slight aversion to gelled concoctions. Too many savory aspic dishes in my childhood.

PPS: Did you really read all of the directions first, or did you just skim?

YIELD: One perfectly lovely Tarte aux Fraises

PULLING OUT THE "GOOD" SILVERWARE
JUST LIKE MOM

During my third hour of weeding, I said to myself, "And I thought this was a good idea because… why?"

Not the weeding. No. That was simply part of "the sickness" as my hubby refers to it. That along with deciding now would be a good time to take down the cathouse that had been sitting unused, out-of-sight since our kitty went up to the Happy Hunting Grounds a year ago. That and deciding now would be a good time to clean out the crawl space under the house, which held such relics as a Princess Palace tent, a puzzle alphabet mat, and foam that was going to be used for window seat cushions in a different house twelve years ago.

No. All of those things were just symptoms of my entertaining sickness (aka The Crazy Projects Carrie Deems Necessary to Complete Before Hosting a Party at Her House Whether or Not the Effort is Directly Related to the Party at Hand).

The cause was deciding to auction off Cooking with Carrie events months ago (as if I'm Rachael Ray, for crying out loud) to be held at my home during the month of April. Now here it was April and I was tired. The incessant gray weather wasn't helping my energy level. And the end of my to-do list seemed to never end.

I forced myself not to think too far in advance. To simply keep going. To check one thing off my list at a time. Weeding – check. Wine glasses labeled – check. Groceries purchased – check. Heavenly little handcrafted chocolate bars tied with raffia – check.

Rain boots on, clippers in one hand, bucket in the other, I headed into my backyard the day before the party. The sun miraculously came out, adding a shimmer to the outside world as it reflected off the raindrops still clinging to the trees. As I clipped the branches, my thoughts turned to my mom. Everything about spring reminds me of her — the daffodils, the purple hyacinths, the different shades of green, the sweet cherry blossoms, the brighter days.

My mom is beautiful. And yes, she's beautiful on the outside but what I'm really talking about is inside. She's a bit like spring herself. Just when you can't take another day of rain, there she is providing you with much-needed bits of color. And not in any loud, pomp and circumstance sort of way, but subtly. Subtle in the way that when you are with her, she's fully present. She listens. Really listens. She gives you and your thoughts a feeling of importance. And you feel your spirits lifted after you've been with her.

I set the table with the good plates, the good glasses, and the good silverware. I used the linen napkins, tablecloth, and runner. Standing back to admire the table, I once again thought of my mom. The way she always sets a beautiful table for us. The ways she clips fresh flowers from her yard and thoughtfully places them on her table and around the house. The way she lights the candles, turns on the music, and brings us all together for a family dinner. Again, her quiet yet thoughtful gestures give us all a feeling of importance. We mean so much to her that she takes the time to create a lovely setting for our meal.

Twenty minutes before my first party, I was ready for my guests. Cesaria Evora was playing in the background. The comforting aroma of candles burning warmed my house. The cherry tree branches were so beautiful inside my home that it didn't matter it had started to snow outside… in April.

In that moment, I realized why I had done all of this. Because with this busy life I lead, I don't take the time to do this very often. To dress up my home and invite people in. To share a meal. To spend a couple of hours getting to know new people. Learning more about friends I already cherish. Passing along what I know and love about cooking so they can go home and do the same for their families. And hopefully, if only for an hour or two, I make them feel important. Extra cared-for.

At the end of my last party, as the final guest walked down the drive, I heard her kindly remark to no one in particular, "I feel like I've died and gone to heaven."

I smiled as I closed the door and said quietly, "Thank you, Mom, for teaching me how to do this."

CHERRY AND ALMOND CAKE

When I was deciding what to serve my guests for dessert, I looked to what was in season and here in Oregon, after five straight months of rain, there's not much in season. A few apples still holding on, some citrus coming up from California, and rhubarb. So, I decided to look for ingredients on the shelves of my pantry. The dried cherries and almonds I found were the perfect inspiration for this modest cake.

3/4 cup whole almonds

1 1/4 cup all-purpose flour

1 teaspoon baking powder

1/2 teaspoon salt

4 large eggs

1 cup sugar

1 1/2 sticks of unsalted butter, melted and cooled

1/3 cup milk

1/4 teaspoon almond extract

1/2 cup chopped, dried cherries

1/2 cup sliced almonds

Optional: confectioner's sugar

Preheat your oven to 350°F. Toast your whole almonds on a cookie sheet for 8 to 12 minutes or until lightly browned and fragrant. Let cool completely. Lightly toast your sliced almonds for 4 minutes.

Butter and flour a 9-inch cake pan. Or if you're like me and don't own a cake pan, flour and butter a deep pie plate.

Put your whole almonds in a food processor and pulse the machine until the nuts are finely ground. Transfer the nuts to a medium bowl. Add your flour, baking powder, and salt. Stir to combine. Set aside.

In a medium bowl, using an electric mixer, beat the eggs and sugar just until combined. Mix in the butter, milk, and almond extract. Stir to combine. Slowly add in your dry ingredients until incorporated. With a wooden spoon or spatula, stir in the cherries. Pour the batter into your prepared cake (or pie) pan. Evenly sprinkle the sliced almonds over the top. Bake for 45 to 50 minutes or until golden on top and a toothpick inserted in the middle comes out clean. Cool on a wire rack. Loosen the edges with a knife. Flip the cake out onto the wire rack and then back over onto a cake stand. Take a few steps back to admire your heavenly creation. Slice and serve while still a bit warm. Enjoy.

YIELD: One 9-inch cake best enjoyed after your party in a silent house with a cup of tea and your slippers on

THE REAL REASON CLEANING OUT
IS OVERWHELMING

Yes, I'm a weeper. Sappy holiday commercials, movies involving orphaned children, and replays of a missed championship shot can all bring on tears. Just this morning, I started weeping while making the kids' lunches. One may have thought it was because of the school lunches that I was weeping. Could have been, but no.

I started thinking about how I'll have a daughter in high school next year and unexpectedly, my eyes filled with tears. Only four years left. Upon seeing me in my emotional state, Hanna gave me a little hug, sighed and said, "Oh, Mom…" and then went back to primping. The eleven-year-old shook his head and the six-year-old reminded me how he'll still be here.

Lately, I've also found myself weepy with all of the spring cleaning and organizing I've been doing.

Yesterday, as I backed my car up to the donation center, I found a lump in my throat as I handed over the foam, muti-colored alphabet mat (that I never liked). I blinked back tears as the Princess Party Tent was handed over (even though I cursed that thing every time I had to set it up). A wave of nostalgia hit me as I pulled out the bag of pixel blocks that no one ever played with but I'd been holding onto for years because someone might.

I'm starting to think that the reason organizing and cleaning out can feel so overwhelming isn't the actual organizing and cleaning out but the letting go.

Once I returned home, however, I felt lighter. Like a little weight had been lifted. I haven't missed the mat, tent, and blocks once…until now as I'm typing this. Now, I'm blinking back tears.

Plenty of parents cry when getting rid of long forgotten toys. But sometimes I even find myself weeping when I face my fridge and try to figure out what to make for lunch or dinner. Sometimes just the thought of cooking again can make me weep, even though I like to cook. But I encourage myself to stand back from the fridge and observe the contents. I know that with all the little bits here and there, I should be able to pull something together.

And then, behind the apples rolling around, I find a crumpled paper sack full of mushrooms. They look a bit weary but they will perk up nicely when sliced up and sautéed with shallots. Back there behind the lettuce is a forgotten bundle of asparagus. It might be a little wilted on the tips, but cut up and combined with the mushrooms, the shallots, and a garlic clove or two, they'll brighten right up. A plastic container of leftover chicken will ground the dish and from myriad half-used bags in my pantry I can pull together enough pasta for our meal.

As I sit there with my family, eating our dinner of bits and pieces that needed to be cleaned out and used up, I feel a little lighter.

And I won't be weeping, but simply enjoying, unless of course you remind me that my daughter is going to high school next year which I just reminded myself by typing it and then, well, I might start weeping...again.

A LITTLE SAUTÉ OF MUSHROOMS
AND ASPARAGUS OVER PENNE

I realize we're almost to the end of asparagus season, but I had to share this quick yet scrumptious dish before those little green shoots disappear until next season. I've made this with various mushrooms and herbs, all with great success. Leftover chicken, some grilled fish, or a sprinkling of pancetta on top could make it a one-dish wonder. Pair it all up with a crisp white wine and you're set.

1 tablespoon butter

2 tablespoons extra-virgin olive oil

1 medium shallot, peeled and diced

2 cloves garlic, peeled and minced

1/2 pound mushrooms, sliced, 3 to 4 cups, white, cremini, or shiitake

1 bundle of asparagus, 3 to 4 cups, cut into one-inch pieces

1/4 cup fresh basil, chopped, or leaves from 4 sprigs of thyme, depending on what's in season

Pinch of red pepper flakes

1/2 teaspoon coarse salt, or to your liking

Fresh black pepper to taste

1 cup pasta water

1/4 cup half and half

1 pound of your favorite pasta - penne, fettuccini, rigatoni

Optional: shredded chicken or crisped pancetta to serve on top

Optional: grated Parmesan cheese

Fill a large pot with water, a sprinkle of salt, and set over high heat to boil. Follow instructions on package for cooking your pasta. Make sure to reserve 1 cup of the pasta water before draining.

In a large skillet over medium heat, melt your butter and heat your olive oil. Add your shallots. Sauté for 2 to 3 minutes. Add in your mushrooms and garlic and sauté another 3 minutes or so. Add in your asparagus, basil or thyme, red pepper flakes, salt and pepper. Sauté another 4 minutes or until your asparagus is cooked to your liking.

Stir in your reserved pasta water and half and half. Let gently simmer for just a few minutes. Spoon over your pasta. Enjoy.

YIELD: Serves 4 as a main dish but 6 to 8 as a side dish

IS IT MY PASSION
OR HERS?

My daughter was three years old when she performed in her first dance recital: "Twinkle, Twinkle, Little Star" and "The Bunny Hop." Her feet could be heard tap, tap, tapping away as she practiced for her big debut. Considering that when she wasn't dancing she was impersonating Mary Poppins, she seemed destined for life as a performer.

On the soccer field, she was the one with bows in her hair, picking daisies, twirling around as the ball rolled past her. When the other players and the competitiveness of the game grew to such a level that skipping as the ball rolled past you wasn't considered cute anymore, my hubby and I decided to pull her from soccer. We encouraged her to forge her own path in dance. And dance, she did… ballet, pointe, jazz, hip-hop, tap, lyrical. Six nights a week. She blossomed into an amazing dancer. And call me biased, but I love to watch her dance. She's captivating on stage.

Just when there seemed to be no end to her dancing days and at the height of sequins, sparkles, Lycra, stage make-up, and dark auditoriums, Hanna said to me, "Mom, I'd really like to try lacrosse."

Like a needle being ripped across a record, the room went silent.

"Lacrosse?"

"Yeah, my friends who play are always telling me how fun it is."

"But, sweetie, you have to wear goggles…and a mouth guard," I said to my fashion-conscious daughter.

"I know."

"And you have to get in there and mix it up with sticks and a ball," added her dad. "You don't like competitive contact. Remember when you played soccer?"

"No, I don't remember. Last time I played I was like in fourth grade."

That was probably true. While her out-in-the-field-picking-daisies ways were still very present in our minds, for her it was four years ago. Almost a third of her life.

We continued to throw out reasons why lacrosse wouldn't work for her and she continued to come back with reasons why it would. On her own, she worked out a schedule that would accommodate lacrosse, dance, and school. She contacted coaches about getting on the team. She figured out how to get to and from practices. When game time came around, she not only got in there and mixed it up, she was aggressive. And fast.

When she asked to go to a tournament in Seattle at the end of the season, we said no. "You are committed to your dance classes that conflict with the lacrosse practices. Your recital is coming up. You can't miss class. Other dancers are counting on you."

She contacted the coaches for the tournament and arranged to miss Monday night practices so she could be at dance. I told my hubby that her determination should be rewarded, so we agreed to let her go to the tournament.

Her team played three games in the tournament. Her dad and I watched every one from under umbrellas and fleece blankets. We watched our daughter fly down the field in the rain, fight for the ball amidst a swarm of sticks, and on occasion put that little ball into the net to score.

Her team lost all three games. The final game had a score of 2-13 but her coach awarded her "Player of the Game" for her persistence and hard work, and I felt myself tear up.

There is something so gratifying about watching your child succeed at something that she alone wanted. Something she was determined to do even if her parents were trying to talk her out of it.

Last week, instead of feeling bitter about driving her to a lacrosse camp across town, with only time to throw together this stand-by soup, I was happy to do it.

And as she shuffled into her dance recital over the weekend, I could tell by her demeanor that this phase of her life was coming to a close. She was still beautiful on stage but there was something removed about her stance. And when I asked her if she thought she'd take dance next year, Hanna said to me, "Well, I know you like me to do dance…"

That's when I told myself, "Let go."

I don't know whether her future will hold mouth guards or ballet slippers, but I do know that it is her future and I love watching her decide for herself just what that future will be.

HAM AND WHITE BEAN SOUP WITH THYME

I know, I know, I'm a year-round crazy soup maker. I find soup to be the perfect one-pot meal when I don't have time to think of anything else. For this soup, I like to soak white flageolet beans overnight, but do you have to do that? No. You can use canned beans, which is what I do most of the time. If using dried, do you have to use flageolet? No. You can use cannellini, some type of bean mix or generic small white beans. Whatever suits your fancy. The bonus of using dried beans is that they tend to hold up better in soup and not get so mushy, but it's not a deal breaker. I get my ham at the deli counter and ask them to slice it thickly. My whole family loves this soup and I serve it with Sicilian bread — basically a rustic loaf with toasted sesame seeds all over the outside.

2 cups dried white beans, or three 15-oz. cans white beans

2 tablespoons olive oil

1 small onion, chopped

1/2 teaspoon dried thyme

2 carrots, peeled, diced

2 stalks celery, diced

1 quart chicken broth

1/2 pound cured ham, cut into cubes

1 teaspoon salt

1/4 teaspoon black pepper

A 1-inch piece of Parmesan cheese rind

More grated Parmesan cheese for on top

If using dried beans, soak them overnight or from early morning until late afternoon, in a bowl with about 3 times as much water as beans. When ready to use, drain and rinse. (Note: I've also gone through the process of soaking them, having dinner plans change and not using them. I simply drain them and put them in the fridge to use the following day. They worked just as well.)

In a large soup pot, sauté your onions in the olive oil for about 5 minutes. Add your carrots, celery and thyme and sauté another 3 to 5 minutes. If using canned beans, drain and rinse them. Add your beans to the pot along with your chicken broth, piece of Parmesan cheese rind, and enough water to cover the beans by 1½ inches.

Bring to a boil. Reduce heat and simmer for 30 minutes if using the dried beans and 20 minutes if using canned.

Add your ham cubes, salt, and pepper and simmer another 15 minutes if using dried beans and 10 minutes if using canned. If using dried, check to make sure they are cooked through. If not, simmer another 10 minutes or so.

That's it. Makes great leftovers for when there isn't any time to cook. Enjoy.

YIELD: One big pot full

BROTHERLY BONDING…
KIND OF

Mom, it's so embarrassing! Do you know what he does all day at school?"

"No, please tell me."

"He skips."

"Well, he's in kindergarten."

"Well, it's embarrassing. My class was lined up to go into the gym and guess who came out of the bathroom and skipped past my whole class and all the way down the hall?"

This eldest son of mine, Jack, then proceeds to go through a litany of infractions committed by his younger brother, Will. "He makes weird noises. He hums. He kicks my seat. He takes my LEGO® guys without asking. He follows me around at recess with his hands like binoculars. He barks at me with those stuffed dogs. And…he skips!"

I did not grow up with brothers. Brothers, plural, that is. I have a brother. My "little" brother. He had the distinct honor of being a worthy subject on which to practice my mothering skills. And that was it. I was more Mommy Jr. to him than sibling rival. And so now, when confronted with this up-close sibling rivalry between brothers, I sometimes feel at a loss as to what to do.

"Just stop it! Stop it!!"

Hearing the screams and crying from the garage, I leave the kitchen (where I've been trying to make and eat a quick salad for lunch) and head out to investigate. Upon seeing me, my kindergartner cries out, pointing in the direction of his older brother, "He threw a basketball at my legs."

In defense, the fifth grader shoots back, "Yeah, well, I wasn't even doing anything and he did this to me."

Jack then proceeds to put his thumbs in his ears, wiggle his fingers, and stick out his tongue. Choking back a smile, I think to myself, "I thought they only did that on TV," but judging by the way Will is covering his face with his arms, apparently my children do that as well.

Both boys look at me as if to say justice must be done. Not sure what to do, I think back to a peace-making method Jack's kindergarten teacher used and enact my own version of it.

"Okay boys, come here. Closer. Face each other. Hold each other's hands."

"No."

"Hold each other's hands and look at each other."

Jack rolls his eyes and grabs his brother's hands. The littler one opens his eyes wide like a zombie, grabs his brother's hands and then proceeds to jump up and down, over and over, like a kangaroo.

"Now I want you to compliment each other. Say something kind about your brother."

This is not a new concept to them. During our family dinners on Sundays (when they actually happen), we take turns complimenting other family members. I can usually count on the fifth-grader to come up with a little gem about his siblings.

"Come on, guys. We're not leaving 'til you say something kind to each other."

"He's not holding my hands," Will cries out.

"Stop jumping! That's so weird," Jack shoots back.

Finally, there is a moment of calm and a bit of silence. I can see the older brother gathering his thoughts; the littler one is no longer jumping but is still wide-eyed, not knowing what to say.

"C'mon. Surely you can think of something," I say, looking at Jack, hoping he'll set a good example.

"Okay, okay," Jack says.

And then, holding his little brother's hands and looking deep into his eyes, he says with all sincerity, "Brother…your farts don't stink."

Will's eyes grow even bigger. He starts jumping again and with a huge smile on his face, he fires back, "Yeah, well…your poop doesn't stink!"

They both start cracking up. I try to stifle my smile, throw my hands up in defeat, and head inside to finally eat my lunch.

While I sit at the kitchen table enjoying the first of this season's strawberries, Jack walks through the kitchen and I say to him, "You know, you'll never be in school with him again in your whole life. You two could grow up to be best of friends but it depends on how you treat each other now. You're going to miss having him around next year."

He continues walking past me but I can tell he's listening. At the foot of the stairs, he says back to me, "I know I'll miss him."

And then further up the stairs, "But I won't miss the skipping!"

A STRAWBERRY, HAZELNUT, AND GOAT CHEESE SALAD DRIZZLED WITH A BIT OF BALSAMIC VINAIGRETTE

I have been reading about pairing sweet, luscious strawberries with piquant balsamic vinegar for quite some time now and I thought it would be fun to try them out in a salad together. Sprinkle on some tangy goat cheese and nutty hazelnuts and you've got a salad fit for a queen, or at least fit to keep you seated long enough to ponder the intricacies of sibling rivalry and what to do about it.

1 tablespoon balsamic vinegar

1 teaspoon shallot, minced

Pinch o' salt

2 to 3 tablespoons olive oil

A couple handfuls of baby greens

1/2 cup or so of sliced strawberries

A sprinkling of crumbled goat cheese (feta might be good too)

A sprinkling of roasted hazelnuts (or walnuts, almonds, whatever nuts you have on hand, and I don't mean your children)

Freshly ground black pepper

Combine your vinegar and shallots in a small bowl and let rest for 5 to 10 minutes. Add your salt and whisk together. Then slowly, while whisking, drizzle in your olive oil. Divide your baby greens between two plates. Top with the strawberries, the goat cheese, and the nuts. Drizzle on the balsamic vinaigrette to your liking. Add a few cracks of black pepper.

Along with your salad, have a couple slices of baguette with salted butter and a glass of sparkling water, all of which will help draw summer near, although that may be hard to fathom for those of us in Portland who some years don't get a spring, but nonetheless, I suggest giving it a try. Enjoy.

YIELD: A salad built for two

KEEPIN' IT SIMPLE TO
SURVIVE PARENTHOOD

At 6:00 a.m. my alarm blares, but I don't budge. Gone are the mornings when I sprang from my bed, tiptoed downstairs, and pedaled my legs around the elliptical for an half hour. This particular morning, I can barely exert the energy to roll over and whack the alarm, sending it into snooze mode, which I do every 20 minutes for the next hour.

At 7:00 a.m., I hoist myself out of bed, open the doors into my sleeping children's rooms, and holler out, "Good morning. Time to get up," as I lumber down the stairs to face the school lunch routine.

Last week, my fifth-grader, Jack, told me about his need for a nap...during school. He convinced some buddies to turn the pages of his book during quiet reading time while he snoozed. Normally, I would have launched into some big lecture on the importance of school, of getting to bed early, of how crucial reading skills are for success in life but instead, I looked at him with fascination and said, "Well, I guess everyone has his methods."

This past weekend, we were enjoying a lovely time on the Oregon Coast. The adults were circled around in beach chairs chatting. The children were splashing in the water, building sand castles, tossing around the lacrosse ball when suddenly, Jack appeared with a bloody lip.

Apparently, he had been hit by an unidentified flying object hurled by his brother. When I asked my kindergartner why he had thrown the object at his brother, Will said with a quivering lip, "He was pressing on my heart!"

I could have launched into a dissertation about how we treat each other or tried the "hold hands and look into each other's eyes" method of reconciliation but instead, I sighed and said, "Well, these things happen."

Recently, I noticed that my daughter, whom I often refer to as "my healthiest eater," had stopped making smoothies for after-school snack. Instead, she was gravitating toward bowls of ice cream. A few days ago, she managed to get a tub of sea salt caramel ice cream into the grocery cart and then proceeded to munch it down, bowl after bowl. Instead of lecturing her about healthy eating and fruits and vegetables, I scooped myself up a bowl and plopped down on the couch to eat it with her, because to bring it full circle...I'm pooped. Which is why not only do I dread making school lunches these days, I dread the dinnertime hour. This is when I must remind myself that not every meal has to be from scratch. It's okay if the chicken and the vegetables did not come from my own backyard. Simple is good.

Sometimes it's enough to just get some form of nourishment on the table and preserve what little energy I have left to enjoy the end-of-the-school-year activities. That flurry of celebrations recognizing a year of hard work — my husband's, the children's, and mine.

SIMPLE STOVE-TO-OVEN SALMON

I believe my love for salmon stems from spending most of my life in the Pacific Northwest. My childhood was spent on boats in Puget Sound fishing for salmon that my father later grilled up with onions and lemon slices. For appetizers, my mother always laid out smoked salmon with cream cheese. Sockeye is my favorite type of salmon and I prefer that it's either fresh or was flash-frozen on the boat that hauled it in.

During the summer, I prefer to grill it but in spring, at the start of salmon season when it's raining outside, I use this stove-to-oven method. Sometimes, when I forget to keep things simple, I make a little compote of shallots and tomatoes to spoon on top.

4 salmon fillets of roughly the same size and thickness

Olive oil

Kosher salt

Freshly ground pepper

Preheat your oven to 450°F. Next, heat a dry, ovenproof sauté pan on the stove over high heat until it's piping hot. I love my cast iron pan for this. Brush all sides of your salmon pieces with olive oil. Liberally season the skinless top and sides with salt and pepper.

When your pan is piping hot, place the salmon fillets, flesh side down, in your pan and let them cook over medium heat for 2 to 3 minutes. Don't move them. Don't touch them. You want to sear the tops of your fillets so they develop a nice crust. Carefully flip your fillets over, trying not to break the crust, then pop the pan in the oven for 5 to 7 more minutes or until the salmon flakes easily with a fork but is still moist. The salmon will continue to cook even when it's out of the oven, so better to pull it out a smidge early rather than too late. Insert a metal spatula in between the flesh and the skin. Your salmon fillet should slip right onto your spatula, leaving the skin behind. Serve with a pot of rice. Enjoy.

YIELD: 4 fillets for 4 people

FORGOT TO KEEP IT SIMPLE TOMATO AND
SHALLOT COMPOTE

2 tablespoons olive oil

2 shallots, peeled and chopped

1 cup cherry tomatoes, halved

1/2 teaspoon kosher salt

Freshly ground pepper

2 sprigs of fresh thyme, leaves removed, stems discarded

Heat the olive oil in a pan. Add the shallots and the salt and pepper and cook over low heat for 5 to 6 minutes or until the shallots are beginning to soften. Add your tomatoes and the thyme leaves and cook another 4 to 5 minutes until softened. Spoon the warm compote on top of your salmon fillets.

YIELD: About 1 cup .

A STRAWBERRY RHUBARB PIE TO HOLD ON TO THE NOISE

I skid down the gravel trail, anxious to enter the canopy of trees — my dome of solitude. I need a break from the noise that comes with the chaos of my life. I jog over the bridge and up the stairs. Deep breath. I've arrived.

I slow my gait and take note of how the forest is filling in. The branches that were bare a few months ago are now decked out in lush green finery; they canopy over the trail. I can no longer make out the stream at the bottom of the trail's steep embankment. The sword ferns have risen up and blocked it from view. But I can hear it.

A few minutes more into my walk, I bump into my neighbor. Usually, I give her a brief wave from the car as I'm taxiing someone somewhere and she's out walking her female golden retriever "of a certain age." But this day, I can actually speak to her in person.

I lamented about the noise in my house and joke about how I can't even hear myself think. She smiles and listens. Her youngest is just about to finish his freshman year at college.

After we finish catching up, I turn away and head down the trail. Before she and her sweet old gal plod up it, she says to me, "I miss the noise."

As I continue on my walk, I think of all the ways my house is quieter than it used to be. I no longer have the incessant babbling, crying, and banging of toys from the toddler and preschool years. The boys spend a lot of their time outside and no longer need my constant supervision. And my daughter, well, she is arranging her own life right now. The one she is growing into and will claim as her own. And often, this "arranging" happens away from home. Which makes me panic and think, "She is leaving for college in three years!"

So, I come home and bake a pie.

I can't stop time any more than I can stop the jowls from forming on the sides of my face. But I can try to slow it down.

I can take the time to combine some flour and butter and press that into a pie plate. I can fill it up with the final bits of spring rhubarb and early strawberries. I can even make a lattice top simply because it's pretty.

I can add a scoop of vanilla ice cream on the side to stand in for the big hug my youngest no longer lets me give him at school. "It's awkward, Mom."

And I can serve it all for breakfast (if it lasts that long) because we aren't much for desserts in the evening, and I never make

breakfast. Pie for breakfast is a novelty. Something different to make them look at me and take notice.

While they eat their breakfast, I look at each one of them. Almost like a hologram, I can see the little girl Hanna once was flashing with the woman she is becoming. Jack, the boy who is just starting his ascent into manhood, has a more pronounced silhouette. And my littlest one has shed his full cheeks but still gives me glimpses of his first few years of life, in the mornings with his sleepy eyes.

And I can continue to eat my pie, in the complete silence of my house, after all of my children have left for school. And I can agree with my neighbor that perhaps I will miss the noise, too.

STRAWBERRY RHUBARB PIE

This might actually be the best pie I have ever made. People inhaled it standing up. Someone left a fork in the pie pan and kept coming back for bites. Someone picked the lattice crust off the top and ate it. There were fights over the last piece. I can't stop thinking about the tiny sliver I got and wishing I had more. Rhubarb is almost on its way out so if you have a hankering to make this, don't wait!

FOR CRUST

2 1/2 cups all-purpose flour

1 teaspoon kosher salt

1 teaspoon granulated sugar

3/4 cup unsalted butter, cold, cut into cubes

1/4 cup shortening, cold

4 to 5 tablespoons ice cold water

FOR THE FILLING

3 1/2 cups strawberries, hulled and sliced (about 2 pints)

3 1/2 cups rhubarb, diced like celery (3 to 4 stalks)

1/2 cup granulated sugar

1/4 cup brown sugar

1/4 cup cornstarch

1 tablespoon lemon juice

1 teaspoon cinnamon

1/2 teaspoon nutmeg

1 large egg

1 tablespoon milk

Optional: sprinkle of coarse sugar

In a large bowl, or the bowl of a food processor, combine your flour, salt, and sugar, either with a whisk or by pulsing a few times. Add in your shortening and butter pieces. Using your fingers or the processor, quickly work the butter into your flour until it begins to looks like cornmeal with a few pea-sized butter pieces sprinkled throughout. If using a food processor, pulse for about 10 seconds to get the same effect. Pour your water in a little bit at a time, working it into your dough just until the dough holds together. If using a food processor, slowly pour your water through the feed tube with the machine running just until dough holds together but not for more than 30 seconds.

Pour your dough out onto a lightly floured surface and quickly form it into a large ball. Divide the dough in half and form two flattened, rounded disks. Wrap them in parchment paper or plastic wrap and put them in the refrigerator for an hour or in the freezer for up to 3 months. Pull your dough out of the refrigerator 10 minutes before using or out of the freezer 30 minutes before.

While your dough is setting, preheat your oven to 400°F and prep your strawberries and rhubarb. In a large bowl, gently combine your strawberries and rhubarb with your granulated sugar, brown sugar, cornstarch, lemon juice, cinnamon, and nutmeg. In a small bowl, whisk together your egg and milk.

On a lightly floured surface, roll out one disk of dough to about 12 inches in diameter and 1/2 inch thick. Gently place it in your 9-inch pie plate. Roll out your second disk of dough to 12 inches in diameter and 1/2 inch thick. If you are interested in trying a lattice top, I recommend an internet search for a how-to video. Carefully pour your filling into the pie plate lined with the first disk of dough.

Gently lift your second rolled-out disk of dough and lay it on top of the filling. Trim the excess dough around the edges of both the top and bottom crust to about ½ inch. Tuck the dough from the top and the bottom under the bottom layer. Using your thumb and pointer finger on one hand and the pointer finger of the other, crimp the edges together to seal the dough. Brush your dough with the egg and milk mixture and sprinkle with coarse sugar. Using a fork or a paring knife, puncture a few air vents into the top dough.

Carefully put your pie on the middle rack of your preheated oven and bake for 20 minutes (put a cookie sheet on the rack beneath it to catch any spills). Turn your oven down to 350°F and cook another 40 to 50 minutes, or until your crust is golden brown and fruit is bubbling. Allow pie to cool for 45 to 60 minutes. Slice it and serve with a scoop of vanilla ice cream. Enjoy!

YIELD: Probably 8 slices unless you have someone standing at the counter eating the whole thing with a spoon, or you're serving a group of ladies who only want a sliver each

FINDING TRANQUILITY
THROUGH DEADHEADING

My mom found tranquility through deadheading. She was always saying, "I'm headed outside to work in the yard." And there she'd go with her gardening gloves, a pair of shears, and an old plastic grocery bag into which she would drop the spent petunia blossoms or the faded roses.

When I was young, I did not have an appreciation for her sanctuary. I couldn't understand why someone would weave a brick walkway to our front door only to flank its sides with purple heather that attracted bees and prevented my eight-year-old self from ever skipping along that path like Dorothy. Instead, I pressed myself flat against the side of my house and sidestepped my way to the driveway where I then sprinted into the cul-de-sac and avoided all contact with my mom's handiwork.

But as I grew older, I started to take notice of her garden. Her hedge of bright blue hydrangeas. The raised bed of cherry tomatoes. Staked raspberry canes along the driveway. Japanese maples, pink azaleas, and star magnolias. The way she tended to her lavender and turned its blossoms into handstiched sachets that are still fragrant years later. And roses. She always grew roses: hybrids, old-fashioneds, and repeat bloomers.

I started accompanying her to nurseries and on garden tours. I began reading Dulcy Mahar's gardening column in *The Oregonian* just like her. I quizzed her on the names of plants as well as their care. I was awed by her encyclopedic knowledge of the botanical world.

During the growing season, she never showed up without little unexpected gifts. A sandwich bag of cherry tomatoes or a few stems of basil, a handful of raspberries or a fragrant bouquet of freshly cut roses — their ends wrapped in a damp paper towel, covered with tin foil and held together with a small plastic bag and a rubber band.

About eighteen months ago, the gravity of my mom's health problems started to become apparent. She was having trouble swallowing. I never would have admitted that the symptoms she was experiencing would lead to her death less than two years later, but in the back of my mind, I knew that something was horribly wrong.

Around that time, my dad went out of town for a couple days. The plan was for me to occasionally check in on my mom. She was still driving and taking care of herself. She could still talk fairly well.

Mid-week, about an hour before I needed to pick up my youngest from school, my phone rang. It was an alarm company. "Hi, we show an alarm going off at the Cook residence. Are you able to tell if this is a false alarm?"

I was thirty minutes away from her house, assuming there wasn't a speck of traffic on any of the highways.

In that pause, between the alarm company asking the questions and me formulating a response, my heart started to race and my mind overloaded with "what ifs." The "what if" my mind settled on was, "What if she choked on something and wasn't able to call for help so she pulled the alarm? I can't get to her quickly enough. She won't make it!"

I explained the situation to the alarm company and had them send out emergency help. I proceeded to pace up and down my kitchen floor, my heart still racing, my breath shallow. Complete panic choked my mind. I called my sister. My brother. "What should I do?" I called the alarm company back. "Did you send someone?" I called the local police station to see if I could get information more quickly. "Is someone at my parents' house? Is my mom okay?" That half an hour of waiting for information felt like years.

And then my cell phone rang. The caller ID was my mom's number.

"Hi, sweetie, I'm sorry I gave you such a scare. The day is so beautiful and after my coffee with the gals, I pulled into the garage and went straight into the backyard. I was deadheading my pots and thinking about what a gorgeous fall day it was when two very handsome young firemen walked into the yard and asked, 'Is everything okay with you, ma'am?' I didn't realize that the garage side door had a silent alarm on it."

She had been out in her garden. How I wished I hadn't disturbed her.

My mom's birthday is this Saturday, May 31st. She would have been 71. I will be spending the day getting my tomato plants in the ground, my petunias and geraniums in pots, and planting roses. While I'm working in the yard, I will be sending up all kinds of birthday wishes to my mom. I can't think of a better way to spend the day with her.

QUINOA SALAD WITH CHERRY TOMATOES AND BASIL
FOR BETTY'S BIRTHDAY

The last five years of my mom's life, in particular, she was a health nut. She was determined to fight her illness and one of the ways she chose to do that was by eating only food that nourished her body. She gave up gluten and became an advocate for quinoa. In my family, I've had a hard time selling quinoa to the kids. I find that it has a rather green, unripened taste to it — more so than the grains we are used to such as wheat. To lessen this grassy taste, I toast my quinoa before I cook it. My mom would have loved this salad, especially using herbs and cherry tomatoes from her garden. Although she would have used balsamic vinegar, her favorite, as opposed to the sherry vinegar I use.

2 tablespoons olive oil

1/4 cup minced shallot

1 cup quinoa

2 cups water

2 cups cherry tomatoes, halved

2 handfuls of fresh spinach leaves

1 handful basil leaves, chopped

1/2 cup feta cheese, crumbled

2 to 3 tablespoons sherry vinegar

1 to 2 tablespoons extra-virgin olive oil

Couple pinches of salt and pepper, to taste

In a medium pot, heat two tablespoons olive oil. Add your shallots and sauté over medium-low heat until softened, about 4 to 5 minutes. Pour in your quinoa and toast for 2 to 3 minutes, stirring often so the quinoa does not burn. Pour in your water. Cover and bring to a boil. Reduce heat and let simmer, covered, about 12 minutes or until all water has been absorbed by the quinoa. Remove from heat and let sit for another 15 minutes. Fluff with a fork and let cool.

In a large bowl, combine your quinoa with the tomatoes, spinach, basil, feta, 2 tablespoons vinegar, 1 tablespoon olive oil, and salt and pepper. Taste. Add the remaining vinegar and olive oil if you feel it needs it. Serve at room temperature. Enjoy!

YIELD: Serves 6 to 8 Homo sapiens

SO IT BEGINS.
AND SO IT ENDS.

As we drove down Broadway toward Seattle's Swedish Hospital, it seemed like we hit every red light. At one point, waiting for yet another light to turn green, I turned to my husband and said, "Gads, when we come back for real, let's take the freeway."

Once we finally arrived and had checked in to the hospital, a nurse strapped all kinds of gizmos on me and then left Dave and me in a semi-dark area with only a bed and one small chair partitioned off from the next patient area by a curtain on a shower rod. We sat there in the dim light not saying much. What could we say? We had no idea how much our lives would change in the 24 hours that followed. We simply listened to the whirring of the machines and my breathing and waited.

After an hour or so, we were startled out of our semi-sleep as the nurse scraped open the shower curtain and announced, "Well, let's get you upstairs. We're having a baby today!"

"Wait, what?" I asked. "My due date's not for another month. I can't be having a baby today. I'm not ready."

"Well, this baby has other plans. She's ready."

My mind quickly flashed to all of the items still left on my pre-baby to-do list: Finish all post-event work from walk-a-thon. Clean the house. Pack hospital bag for me and going-home bag for baby. Find cat and dog sitter. Take breastfeeding class. Buy film for camera. Take a shower!

I thought about how just that morning I had been helping my sister-in-law and brother-in-law move into their new home. As I traipsed up and down the stairs with light boxes, I had to stop and hold onto the railing from time to time due to what I thought were Braxton Hicks contractions. My sister-in-law said to me at one point, "You better not have that baby here." To which I replied, "I'm not going to have this baby now. It's only May 4th. She's not due until May 31st. Remember? My mom's birthday?"

I had been so proud of my creativity eight months earlier when at a birthday celebration for my dad, I had handed my mom a small gift and said, "You get to have a little early birthday gift too."

She unwrapped the gift and pulled out an Eeyore rattle with a note tied onto it that read, "Do not use until May 31st." My mom immediately started screaming happy screams. My dad looked around saying, "What? What?" until his eyes met Dave's and then he said, "Oh!" and they both smiled sheepishly at each other.

Curiously, I didn't cry when Hanna was born a few hours after we had arrived, or even when I held her in my arms for the first time and peeked at her rosebud lips and tiny chin. I didn't even think to bring her to the breastfeeding class the following morning at the hospital. They handed me a doll and then told me to come back again for the afternoon class with my real baby. I shuffled through those first 24 hours in a daze wearing wool socks and a pale pink bathrobe.

The following day, they wheeled me out to my car with all of my belongings, which now included 5 pound 15 ounce Hanna who was tucked into her car seat like a baby doll. Dave drove and I sat in the back peering at sleeping Hanna and pushing down the neck on the preemie-sized outfit that was much too large for her. Dave and I didn't say much to one another. As we waited for those red lights to turn green all the way back down Broadway toward home, the magnitude of what I was about to undertake hit me. I would not only be responsible for caring for this tiny little human, but for raising her up to be a strong, intelligent, and compassionate adult — one who would contribute to society and leave our fragile planet a little better than when she first arrived. I didn't even know where to begin. Slow, warm tears rolled down my cheeks for the rest of our drive home.

Last week, I dropped Hanna off at college. Leaving her there felt akin to ripping my heart out of my chest and tossing it out into rush hour traffic on I-5

as it squeezes its way through downtown Seattle less than a mile from where she was born. After I left her there in the Emerald City and headed back down I-5 to Portland, constant questions ran through my mind as those same slow, warm tears rolled down my face: "Did I do enough? Did I teach her enough? Did I spend enough time with her?"

I'll never know the answers to those questions. I believe I did the best that I could with what I know and who I am. I do believe that I left behind a strong, intelligent and compassionate woman on that college campus. But during the drive home, what I realized for certain was that while I was focused on raising Hanna, she was raising me into the woman who I am now. I've learned so much from her, as well as her brothers, throughout their childhoods. I could write a whole book on what they've taught me about myself and how through their courage to learn, to take risks, to find their own voices and their own paths out into the world, they've given me the courage to do the same in my life.

However, despite all that, I believe the most insightful lesson I've learned from all three of my children is the sobering truth that life goes by so fast. It never stops. It's always changing. It doesn't wait for you to raise your hand or wait patiently in line. It doesn't wait for you to finish the photo albums or plan the perfect family vacations. It barely gives you time to try to figure out the best parenting solution to the current child-rearing situation before the next one hits. It is but a single blink from the drive home from the hospital to the drive home from the college drop-off. Knowing how quickly that blink goes, I'm here to say to you that if there is something you want to do in your life, you must do it now. No matter your age. No matter your education or income level. You must carve out the time as if your life or the lives of your children depended on it.

Because of that knowledge, I have demanded of myself that I find something with purpose that gets me up in the morning, that can help inspire others to do the same, and that leaves a little bit of my singular self here after I'm gone. I believe that I have found that through writing, photography, and food. It is my greatest hope that my children find their own version of that as they make their way through their lives. And I hope you do too.

BETTY'S CELEBRATORY CARROT CAKE

I have never cared for traditional cake nor for the frosting that adorns it. For my birthday parties growing up, my mom often made me the heartier carrot cake or spice cake, which I loved after I'd scraped off the frosting. While I did have a traditional cake at my wedding, in retrospect, I wish I'd served pumpkin pie. Hanna loves cake, and she particularly loves carrot cake with the frosting. So, to celebrate her high school graduation and her send-off to college, I thought it only appropriate that I make her a carrot cake — with the frosting on the side so we're both happy. The recipe that follows is my mom's with a few small changes made by me.

FOR THE CAKE
2 1/4 cups all-purpose flour

11/2 teaspoon cinnamon

1/2 teaspoon nutmeg

1 teaspoon baking soda

1 teaspoon baking powder

1/2 teaspoon salt

1 cup canola oil

2 cups sugar

4 eggs

1 teaspoon vanilla

3 cups grated carrots

Optional: 1 cup walnuts, chopped

FOR THE FROSTING
1 cup butter, softened

1 8-oz. package cream cheese, softened

1 16-oz. box of confectioner's sugar (about 4 cups)

1 teaspoon vanilla

Preheat oven to 350°F. Grease and flour a 10-inch Bundt pan.

In a medium bowl, stir together your flour, cinnamon, nutmeg, baking soda, baking powder, and salt. Set aside.

In a large bowl, beat together your oil, sugar, eggs, and vanilla with an electric mixer until well combined (about a minute). With the mixer on low, slowly pour in your flour mixture until just combined. Using a spoon, fold in your carrots and your nuts (if using). Pour batter into your prepared Bundt pan and bake for 45-60 minutes or until a toothpick inserted in the middle comes out clean. Place on a cooling rack and let cool completely before removing from pan.

While cake is baking, whip together your frosting ingredients — butter, cream cheese, confectioner's sugar, and vanilla — until smooth and creamy. Refrigerate frosting when not using.

Once cake is cooled and removed from pan, dust lightly with confectioner's sugar. Slice and serve with cream cheese frosting on the side. Enjoy!

YIELD: One fairly large carrot cake

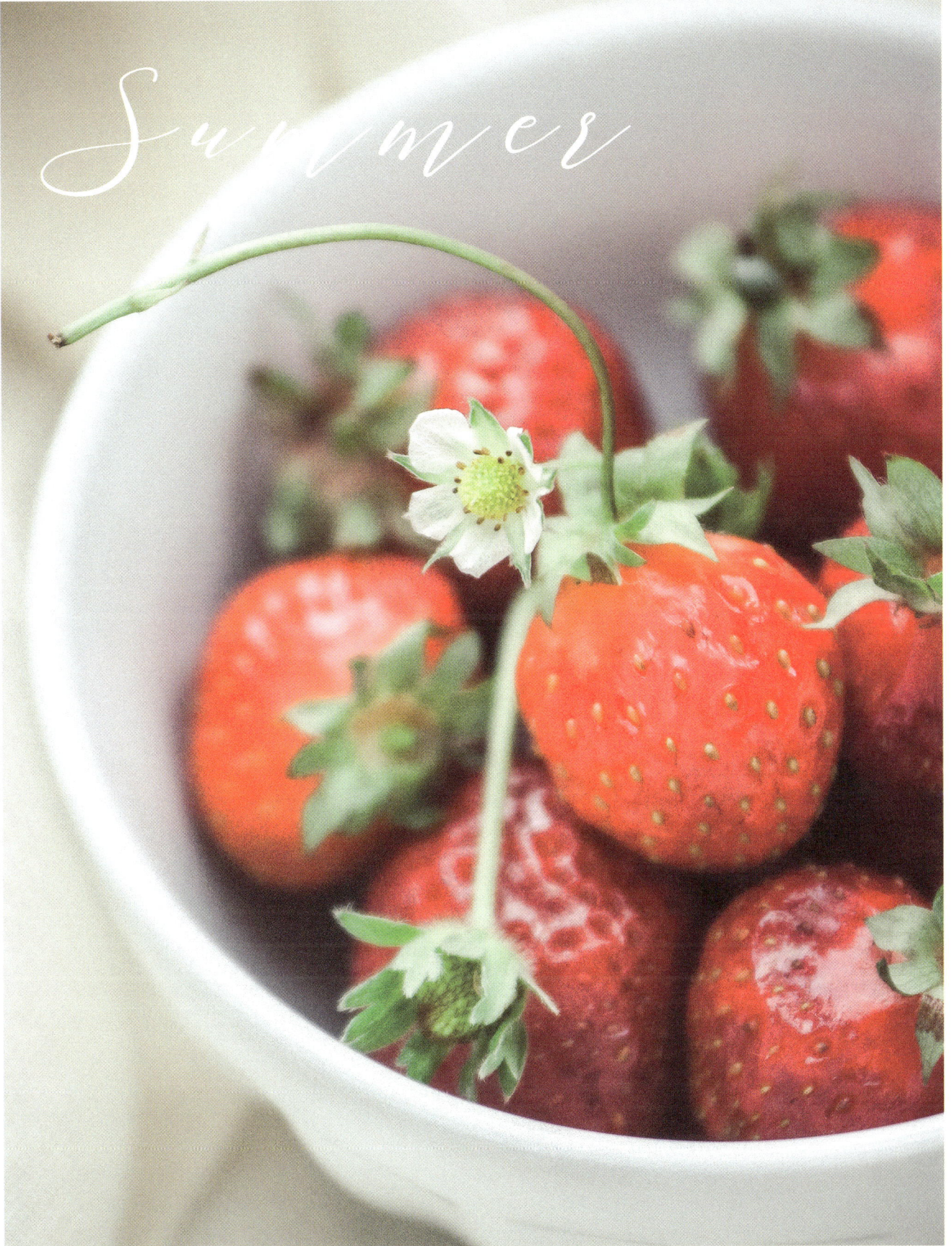

Summer

THE PLUSES OF DO-IT-YOURSELF PAINTING

I snap open the navy and white striped sheet and watch the swath of material flutter to the ground. For a brief moment, I am transported back to the first apartment I shared with my hubby, where this simple sheet rested prominently on our bed. The same apartment where our cat, Bruce, a mere kitten at the time, decided to skydive off our third floor balcony and quickly used up one of his lives. The same apartment where I decided to can salsa for Christmas gifts, using a recipe I'd never tried nor bothered to taste during the creating. The salsa did not become a tradition. Perhaps it was the Worcestershire sauce.

Another snap of a sheet and this time it's a Florentine marbled design in peaches, soft blues, and pale pink. I can see the bed in my college room where this sheet started out. I can see it in its final resting place on a twin bed in the guest room of our little walk-up in San Francisco's Noe Valley neighborhood, where I threw a 30th birthday party for my sweetie while suffering from the flu. The same party that included the chef and owner of our San Francisco neighborhood's Italian restaurant. When a metallic smell started emanating from the oven, it was he who discovered that I had failed to remove the plastic protector from underneath my new pizza stones. He yanked the noxious pizzas from the oven as a trail of hot plastic oozed behind him like pulled taffy.

A flash of pink and white check, and it's the sheet from my daughter's first bedroom. Ballet pink. Baby dolls and handmade cradles. Dress-up clothes and a kitchen. Fish sticks, peas, and applesauce. The swath of material softly falls to the ground and takes up its place next to the others. Together they make up my painting quilt that protects the floor as I cover the ballet-pink walls with each stroke of the brush.

In our 30s, we often leave our painting days behind and hire it out, but allow me to say a few words in favor of do-it-yourself painting. For starters, it's cathartic. Relaxing. The mesmerizing sound of the brush against the wall. Painting is very deliberate. You have to slow down. Be careful. Don't splatter. You find yourself alone with your thoughts. To consider that the daughter who once wrapped herself in every shade of pink imaginable is no longer that little girl. With each stroke of the brush you recognize that she is growing up. Her walls are becoming a fresh, creamy white. And while there is some tug at your heart, knowing that the little girl will never be again, you can't help but be excited for what lies ahead.

With each passing day, you are able to shed little bits of your role as parent. And one day, should you do your job well, you will shed enough of the parent role to be her friend. So you say good-bye to the ballet pink and the subtle chain of daisies you stenciled round the room years ago.

I pick up my cup of chamomile and mint tea and gaze outside at the gray skies and 64-degree weather. Not an uncommon summer day in Portland. I reach down to the ramekin of granola I've been munching on all morning while pondering the passing years. Oats, coconut, seeds, cinnamon, a pinch of salt and a dollop of maple syrup all roasted to a nutty perfection. And I pause to consider that while I had been painting over her little girl walls, my almost teenage daughter had been roasting up this delectable concoction. And there's another reason in favor of do-it-yourself painting. When you tell the kids that you will be unavailable for the day due to the painting project, and that they will be in charge of their own snacks and their own meals, they take you seriously. And you become the happy benefactor of their newly independent ways.

HANNA'S DO-IT-YOURSELF GRANOLA

A straightforward recipe for a healthy snack that your pre-teen kids can make for you. Everyone in my house loves this recipe so we tend to double it. I leave it sitting in an airtight container on the counter and next to it are little jars of mix-ins: dried fruit, toasted nuts, chocolate chips. A buffet!

1 pound rolled oats (3 cups) (I use gluten-free oats)

1 cup unsweetened, shredded coconut (I use Bob's Red Mill)

1/4 cup light brown sugar

1 teaspoon coarse salt

1 teaspoon cinnamon

1/4 teaspoon nutmeg

1/4 cup mixture of your favorite seeds: flax, chia, sesame, poppy, sunflower

1/4 cup coconut oil

1/4 cup olive oil

1/2 cup maple syrup

1 teaspoon vanilla

Preheat oven to 300°F (or, for convection, 275°F)

In a large mixing bowl, combine rolled oats, coconut, brown sugar, salt, cinnamon, nutmeg, and seeds. Mix to combine. Set aside.

In a small saucepan, melt coconut oil over low heat. Remove from heat. Stir in olive oil, maple syrup, and vanilla.

On a large jelly roll pan (a cookie sheet with 1-inch raised sides), spread your granola in an even layer. Bake for 35 to 40 minutes, or until golden brown on the top (30 to 35 minutes for convection.) Sometimes I take it out every 10 to 15 minutes and stir it. Other times, I simply don't feel like fussing with it and don't stir it at all.

Mix-in ideas: coarsely chopped unsweetened cherries, raisins, toasted nuts like almonds, pecans, or walnuts, chocolate chips, yogurt, milk, and/or ice cream.
Enjoy!

YIELD: Enough to last for a few days on the counter with people walking by and grabbing a handful from time to time

A TOAST FOR SEEMINGLY
SMALL THINGS

For years, my children pleaded for a vegetable garden complete with not just lettuce but tomatoes, carrots, beans, and zucchini. Earlier this summer, we finally planted one. Of course, once the excitement around choosing the vegetables and planting the seeds died down, I was left alone to tend to my little plot. However, I didn't mind. I find it quite gratifying to see those little green shoots poke their way up out of the dirt's blank canvas. Even more satisfying is tossing together a salad with my homegrown lettuce. Lettuce I didn't have to pay for. Lettuce I didn't have to use the car to acquire. Lettuce that I know has only been sprayed with water.

My potager ticked right along while I looked forward to its bounty. And then, a water leak — one of those household maintenance projects that comes out of nowhere and scoots itself right to the top of the to-do list. Directly beneath the leak sat my garden. During the next few weeks, I watched as my tomato plants bravely stretched their arms, baring their little yellow flowers and green globes. The zucchini put out its cheery orange blossoms and decided to climb over the side. The beans bailed on the trellis and scampered all over the ground. Meanwhile, a hailstorm of sawdust and debris tumbled down onto my plants. Men on ladders climbed up and over them. Branches were broken. Their green leaves appeared to be covered with snow. And yet, even at the worst of it, when I could hardly bear to watch, I'd peek out from behind the curtain and somehow they were still there. Growing. Thriving.

I reaped my first harvest yesterday: a tiny zucchini, some cherry tomatoes, a handful of green beans. Not much, but still, it's something. After I gave them a good washing off, I popped a few cherry tomatoes into my mouth. I wasn't sure what to expect, considering that their growing environment had been less than ideal. But they were perfect: Sweet. Luscious. Juicy. And still warm from the sun.

But, as often happens here in Portland, even in the summer, the warm morning sun was blotted out by rain clouds. What should have been an afternoon full of sprinklers became an afternoon that sent everyone indoors, putting on wool socks and pining away for soup. Usually, I don't make soup until the kids are back in school, but considering that I had fresh green beans and the weather had turned gloomy, I went ahead.

While I cut up my onions and carrots, I sipped a glass of pinot noir in honor of my father-in-law who passed away a year ago on this day. His favorite Herb Alpert and the Tijuana Brass played in the background. I found myself lost in my remembrances of him and surrounded by the warm, swirling smells of sautéed onions.

I set down on the worn kitchen table steaming bowls of our vegetable soup, a plate of blackberries and yellow peaches, sliced ciabatta bread, and remnants of cheese pieces I found in the fridge. As my family ate the meal created from our harvest, we talked about Grandad. His smile. His quiet laugh. His humming. His ability to thrive in less than ideal situations. His love for his grandkids. And, as my sweetie put it, his gratitude for seemingly small things. So please, if you will, raise a glass for Grandad, his genuine gratitude, and the pleasure of the harvest no matter how small, no matter how dusty.

RAINY DAY VEGETABLE SOUP

The great thing about a vegetable soup is that the quantities below are just guidelines. If you don't have celery, fine. If you need to use up two cups of green beans before they go to waste instead of one, great. If you want to use basil and oregano instead of thyme and bay leaves, fantastic.

FOR THE SOUP

2 tablespoons olive oil

1 medium yellow onion, peeled and diced

1 cup carrots, diced

1 cup celery, diced

2 garlic cloves, peeled and minced

2 medium zucchini, diced

1 cup green beans, cut into 1" pieces

2 medium red- or white-skinned potatoes, cubed

2 teaspoons Herbes de Provence, or 6 sprigs fresh thyme and 2 bay leaves

1/2 teaspoon salt

1/2 teaspoon freshly ground black pepper or to taste

1 28-oz. can diced tomatoes

2 quarts chicken broth

1 15-oz. can cannellini beans or any other can of white beans you have lying around, drained and rinsed

A handful of small pasta — alphabet, orzo, broken spaghetti pieces

Optional but recommended: 1 inch piece of Parmesan cheese rind

FOR THE PISTOU
1 cup fresh basil leaves

2 garlic cloves, peeled

1/8 cup tomato paste

1/4 cup grated Parmesan cheese

1/8-1/4 cup extra virgin olive oil

In a large soup pot, warm your olive oil over medium heat. Add your onions and sauté 5-6 minutes, or until the onions start to soften and turn translucent. While your onions are sautéing, dice up your carrots and celery. Add them to the pot, sauté for an additional 5-6 minutes. Mince up your garlic. Add it to the pot and sauté for one more minute.

Next, put your zucchini, green beans, potatoes, Herbes de Provence or thyme and bay leaves, salt, and pepper in the pot. Stir the medley together. Pour in your tomatoes and your broth. Drop in your Parmesan cheese rind and bring the whole concoction to a boil. Then, reduce the heat and simmer 20-25 minutes.

While your soup is simmering, make the pistou. First, combine the basil and garlic using a mortal and pestle. Or, using the backside of a serving spoon, mash the basil and garlic on your cutting board. Next, grind in the cheese and tomato paste. Drizzle the olive oil on top and stir it all up.

Once your buzzer goes off for the soup, add your beans and pasta, bring to a boil, reduce heat, and simmer for another 10 minutes. Pull out the cheese rind and the bay leaves; discard. Ring the cowbell to call everyone to the kitchen for dinner. Have them ladle the summer harvest soup into shallow bowls and top with a small scoop of pistou straight off the cutting board.

Now, as with all things worth waiting for — wine, women, cheese — this soup is delicious the first day but even better the next. As the soup ages, the flavors mingle to give it a depth and complexity it lacks when it's young. So enjoy it for dinner tonight, but appreciate the soup's deeper flavors the following days.

YIELD: Enough for a family of 5, plus leftovers for lunch the next day

SOMETIMES NO MEANS NO
UNTIL IT MEANS YES

When my mother-in-law emailed to say that she was coming to visit us for a week in August, I rejoiced. Contrary to the negative connotation that the words "mother-in-law" usually elicit, I am fortunate to be married to a man whose mother is lovely. When Nanny comes to town, we visit farmers markets together, cook together, drink cabernet together, and in the evening curl up on the couch and chat like dear friends. I rearranged the calendar so the days would be wide open for her visit. Then she reminded me why she was coming.

"On Tuesday, I'll be picking up my golden retriever puppy, Mollie."

Not a day goes by that my children do not beg me for a puppy. Present me with spreadsheets and flowcharts regarding the cost outlay and delegation of responsibilities. Perform award-winning speeches in persuasive speaking. When my ten-year-old was a preschooler, I said that once he was in kindergarten we could get a puppy. Then, along came a real baby and I started saying, "The baby IS the puppy. You can take him for walks, teach him tricks, and even clean his poopy diapers."

This worked…for a while. But Nanny's visit re-opened the puppy campaign.

Wanting to share in the excitement, the whole family piled in the car when Nanny drove out to meet her puppy. We were ushered into the small greeting room where we held Mollie, the World's Cutest Puppy, snuggled her, sniffed her puppy breath, and told her we'd be back for her in a few days. As we were standing up to go it was casually mentioned, "We still have a male puppy available. Would you like to see him?"

And someone said, "Yes."

We held him, snuggled him, sniffed his puppy breath, and said we'd be back for him in a few days.

Driving home, we talked about where he would sleep. What we would name him. We talked about walking him, feeding him, and cleaning up after him. We went to bed elated. At 4:00 a.m., I sat straight up, hurled a few expletives, and said to myself, "Please tell me you did not agree to get a puppy?"

While the rest of the house slept, I wrote my speech. It's not as if we haven't had a puppy before. We had a gentle 80-pound golden retriever in our lives for eight years before he died much too young from cancer. As my mind raced to come up with the most honest reasoning I could give to my children, I realized that during all those years of "not another puppy," I'd been blaming it on my hubby — "You know that Daddy doesn't want a dog" — when the real reason lay with me.

Mid-morning, I gathered the children on our bed, took a deep breath and said, "We can't get the puppy. And here's why. When Daddy and I decided to have children, I wanted my full-time job to be at home with you, raising you, watching you grow into the amazing people you are. I didn't have to do that, I wanted to. However, for almost 13 years, Mommy's been in the baby phase of parenting and I'm ready for the next phase. I can see it coming. It's almost here and if we get a puppy, that puts Mommy back in the baby phase for at least another two years."

"But we would help!"

"I know that you say you would help and your words are genuine, but the reality is that I would be responsible for the puppy and I can't do it."

"Why?"

"Imagine that you get to go to a beautiful school. Flowers everywhere. A gigantic playground with real swings. You can even play football at recess. And each day that you come to school, you get to study something you love…maybe for you, it's fashion design, and for you, it's sports psychology, and for me, child development. Although you get a break to eat your meals, there isn't any recess. And there aren't any weekends or holiday vacations. And after dinner, you have homework until bed. As the years go by, you begin to look up from your studies long enough to notice that other people are outside playing, swinging on the swings. Other people have recess. And… Mommy wants recess."

I looked at my children. The ten-year-old was staring off into space. The baby was bouncing around our cat, saying, "I just want a black kitty." And my daughter…silent tears tickled down her cheeks. Swallowing the lump in my throat, I quietly said, "I'm so sorry. I wish I could give you this. I love dogs. But I can't take care of one right now."

Later in the week, Nanny sent us an email saying that Mollie had made the cross-country flight just fine. Attached to the email were pictures of Mollie in her new home and a recipe for creamy coleslaw. While I whipped up that coleslaw to put on top of pulled pork sandwiches for dinner, my stomach tightened as I thought about how sometimes the hardest part of being a parent is saying no, especially when the one who benefits most is the mommy.

Four years later, we did bring home a golden retriever puppy and named him Benson. Even though recess is over again, our house is a better place because of this funny and furry family member. Although when I ask my daughter why she doesn't help out more with Benson, she replies, "You waited too long, Mom. I'm out of the dog phase."

PULLED PORK SANDWICHES
WITH TANGY COLESLAW

I love this coleslaw recipe. I have doubled the recipe and brought it to parties where it disappears. I have also made the dressing and then tossed it over a pre-shredded coleslaw mix from the produce department. I've left out the carrots and green onions. I've used only green cabbage. In other words, this recipe is flexible. Store your sesame oil in the refrigerator to extend its life. As for the barbecue sauce, I like to use the different small-batch barbecue sauces I find in my grocery store or at the farmers market.

FOR THE PULLED PORK

4 pounds boneless pork shoulder, twine removed, fat trimmed off

Kosher salt

Freshly ground black pepper

Red chili powder

1 medium yellow onion, peeled and sliced

3 garlic cloves, peeled and sliced

1 cup water

Bottle of your favorite barbecue sauce

FOR THE COLESLAW

1/3 cup plain yogurt

1/3 cup mayonnaise

1 1/2 teaspoons toasted sesame oil

1/8 cup apple cider vinegar

1/2 teaspoon Kosher salt (or whatever salt you have on hand)

1/4 teaspoon black pepper

1/2 head green cabbage, chopped

1/2 head red cabbage, chopped

3 carrots, peeled and grated

One bundle of green onions, chopped or 1/4 cup chives, chopped

Cover the bottom of a large slow cooker with your onion and garlic slices. Rub your pork generously on all sides with salt, pepper, and red chili powder. Place meat in slow cooker, and pour water around the meat. Cook on low for 8-10 hours or on high for 3-5 hours until pork is tender and falling apart.

While meat is cooking, whip up your coleslaw dressing. In a medium bowl, whisk together your yogurt, mayonnaise, sesame oil, apple cider vinegar, salt, and pepper. Set aside in the refrigerator for at least 30 minutes and up to a day so the flavors can meld and soften.

Right before serving, toss your cabbage, carrots, and green onions/chives together in a big bowl. Drizzle with enough dressing to your liking.

Once your meat is done cooking, transfer to a cutting board, let cool slightly and then shred using two forks. Drain the liquid from your slow cooker. Add the meat back in and stir in ½ cup or so of barbecue sauce. Serve the pork with bakery fresh buns, additional warmed barbecue sauce, and your creamy coleslaw to go on top or next to your sandwiches. Enjoy!

YIELD: Enough for a family of 5 plus the grandparents in town for the weekend

WHEN EASY-TO-USE
IS ANYTHING BUT

Usually, I arrived at the farmers market an hour before closing, at the height of the crowds, when many of the vendors were starting to sell out. Not this day. My parking meter ticket confirmed that I had arrived 45 minutes after it had opened. Not only that, the sun was shining for the first time in weeks and I was determined to make the most of the next 24 hours before the rain returned.

Going around to the back of the car, I pulled out a collapsible cart I had purchased online for toting around my bags of produce. I was hoping that it might give my lower back and arms a reprieve during this weekly jaunt. I unfolded it, grabbed my bags, and hung them on the rungs.

"Hmm," I mumbled when I noticed that the bags seemed to drag on the ground once they were hooked. "Oh, I'm sure it will be fine once they're filled with food."

Waving off someone gesturing for my parking spot, I grabbed the cart handle and strode off toward the entrance, looking forward to my calm and relaxing trip around the market.

As I approached the white canopies, I noticed that the walkways were teeming with people. I couldn't believe it. "It's only 9:15. Where did all of these people come from? I'm supposed to have the market to myself."

A flash of disappointment rippled through my body. I like to circle the market once before I buy anything. Check out deals. Inspect the produce. As I dove into the crowd, I could sense that this was not a day for leisurely shopping. No circling. Just grab n' go. As for my new cart, I may as well have been trying to push a doublewide stroller through a mall during the holidays.

First, I stopped at my favorite strawberry stand. While I was inspecting the berries, a lovely couple noticed my new contraption.

"Well, that's an interesting cart. What's it called, darlin'?"

I rattled off the name and explained that it was new. Turning to his wife, the man said, "Honey, we'll have to check that out online."

Back in the crowd, I bought a few more items — a baguette, some sugar snap peas, basil, goat cheese, Pacific rockfish fillets, and a bottle of sauvignon blanc. I plopped them into bag number one.

Rounding the corner, I spied a huge pile of zucchini. I grabbed a few with visions of grilling them with a little olive oil and salt and pepper. After my purchase,

I pulled off to the side to get them into bag number two. Clearly, the handles were too long. The bag would drag once it was hooked. While I was concentrating on tying knots to shorten the handles, another lovely couple walked up to take a look at my cart.

"Well, look at that. What kind of contraption is that?"

"Oh, I'm just trying it out for the first time today."

"Those bags are going to drag."

"Yeah, well, I haven't worked out all the kinks. This is the first time I've taken her out for a spin."

"Shoddy design," the husband muttered as he walked away with his wife following behind.

I wanted to take the zucchini back out of the bag that was not dragging and whack him on the head, but the knot I had tied to shorten the handles prevented me from reaching into the bag.

With my half-flat of strawberries hooked on my arm and my bags hooked on the cart, I headed toward the exit. Before I could break free from the crowds, another lovely couple sidled up beside me. "Miss, you know those bags are dragging on the ground."

Once home, I rushed to unload the car, put away my purchases, and spent the rest of my afternoon pulling weeds. Around 7 p.m., I rang the cowbell to call everyone for dinner. Once seated, I took a deep breath and felt myself relax. I watched as my family enjoyed their fish tacos and chatted about this and that. My sweetie remarked, "These might be the best fish tacos I've ever had."

The sun was starting to disappear in preparation for the next day's rain, but as I sat there with my family I didn't mind. At the end of a long and productive sunny day, I was finally having my calming moment surrounded by my hubby and my curiously calm chickens. The sauvignon blanc probably helped, too. As for my new cart, it might just have to go.

FABULOUS FISH TACOS

Dave and I are always on the hunt for the best fish tacos. This recipe is a conglomeration of many of the fish tacos we've enjoyed. I like to use Pacific rockfish, which was recommended to me by Linda Brand Crab at the Portland Farmers Market. She wasn't just trying to sell fish when she said they'd be perfect for fish tacos. This recipe is so simple. It can easily be made on a weeknight or on the weekend for guests.

1/3 cup mayonnaise	*1 handful cilantro, finely chopped*
1/3 cup sour cream	*Extra slices of lime*
2 tablespoons freshly squeezed lime juice	*2 pounds Pacific rockfish or other firm, fleshy white fish*
1/4 teaspoon cumin	*Olive oil*
1/4 teaspoon chili powder	*Salt and pepper*
Pinch or two of salt	*White corn tortillas*
1/2 head Napa cabbage, shredded	*Optional: Sriracha or chili sauce on the table for those who like a bit of heat*
1-2 mangoes, peeled and diced	

Prepare your sauce by mixing the mayonnaise, sour cream, lime juice, cumin, chili powder, and salt together in a bowl. Set aside in the fridge at least 30 minutes before using to allow the flavors to mingle. Place the prepared cabbage, mangoes, and cilantro on individual plates. Set aside.

Generously brush both sides of your fish with olive oil and season with salt and pepper. Grill over direct medium heat until just flaky in the middle, about 3-4 minutes. Flip once halfway through.

While your fish is grilling, heat your tortillas. An easy way is to wrap the tortillas in a barely damp paper towel and pop them in the microwave for 45 seconds or so. They come out heated through without being dried up. You could also get fancy and warm them individually in a cast iron skillet with a little olive oil for a minute or two on each side.

Lay your fixings out on the counter, pull your fish off the grill, and call the troops to dinner. Instruct them to take a tortilla (or two), put some fish on it, drizzle on some sauce, top with cilantro, mangoes and cabbage, and perhaps a squeeze of lime. Then, after preparing yourself a plate, sit down and enjoy.

YIELD: Enough for 2 adults and 3 children and a bit leftover

BLUEBERRY HAND PIES
TO LIFT THE SPIRITS

Is something the matter? You don't seem yourself," my friend inquired. "I don't know. I feel a little…sad." "Melancholy?" "Yeah, maybe. I'm not sure why." Here it was the end of the school year. A day that I had been looking forward to for months. A day that I had been counting down the minutes until its arrival. Now, here it was and…sigh. I couldn't shake this heaviness. Not wanting to cast a shadow over the end-of-the-year celebration, I tried to perk myself up by clinking glasses of champagne with my friends and tossing out homemade blueberry hand pies to the children before they scampered outside to play.

I should be rejoicing. No more lunches. No more homework. No more wondering whether my daughter would actually get herself ready for school in time to take the bus or would I, once again, be driving her the hour-long round trip? Oh, I know, there are some of you dutiful parents out there thinking that I should teach her a lesson by saying, "If you don't make the bus, then you don't go to school."

But let's think about that one. Will that actually work? Who really suffers from those consequences? And besides, I remember those junior high years — spending hours in the morning on my Farrah Fawcett curls and my electric blue eyeliner.

Being raised in a military family, I grew up saying good-bye a lot. Whether it was our family moving or another family. I also grew up saying good-bye to my own father for months, even years at a time; he always reminded us, "Never say good-bye. Always say, 'I'll see you later.'"

I've tried as best I could to honor the sentiment behind those words, but as more and more time collects behind me, I've come to realize that sometimes, good-bye is good-bye. And the end of the school year, while joyous for so many reasons, can also be a bit melancholy.

It's the end of a chapter. In our lives. Our children's lives. Not everything from that chapter carries forward. We say good-bye to teachers. Amazing, incredible teachers whom we feel inept to properly thank. Teachers who not only taught our children, but genuinely cared about them. Good-bye to that 5th year, that 10th year, that 12th year of our children's lives. Good-bye to a rhythm and tempo that was unique for that one year. And saying good-bye can sometimes be sad.

I left that Last-Day-of-School celebration with my spirits lifted a bit thanks to the champagne and a medley of Journey songs on the stereo. Nothing quite does it for me like a round of *Don't Stop Believin'*. Takes me right back to those curls and the electric blue eyeliner.

And maybe my dad's right. Maybe it is see ya later. Look how *Don't Stop Believin'* shows back up out of nowhere when we thought we'd said good-bye to it a long time ago.

As the days passed, I felt less wistful. I had all of my chickens home. No more schedules. No more daily commitments. Stretched out in front of us was an entire summer of togetherness.

A few weeks into summer, I ran into my local coffee shop to grab a latte. Before I closed the car door, I turned to my eldest son and said, "No taunting or teasing your brother."

Then, I turned to the littlest one, "Do not bite your brother again."

And to both of them, "And you guys… no more wedgies."

I could see them trying to choke back their smiles. As I slammed the door shut, I thought to myself, "And why were you excited for the end of the school year? And why were you sad?"

BLUEBERRY HAND PIES

I know, I know, nobody really loves to read the directions first, but in the case of this recipe, I insist. There is simply too much going on here not to know ahead of time what needs to happen. But oh, once you follow these blasted directions and pull your little pillows of warm butter, cinnamon, and blueberries from the oven, you and everyone around you will swoon at your creation. And then your hand pies will be devoured. Go forth and create, my friend.

FOR THE CRUST
2 1/2 cups all-purpose flour

1 teaspoon coarse salt

1 teaspoon sugar

1 cup (2 sticks) chilled unsalted butter, cut into large diced pieces

1/4-1/2 cup ice water

Have on hand parchment paper cut into 8 x 8 inch squares. You'll need 40 squares.

FOR THE EGG WASH
1 large egg

1 tablespoon water

FOR THE FILLING
1/4 cup cornstarch

1/2 cup granulated sugar

1/4 teaspoon salt

1 teaspoon lemon zest, minced

1/2 teaspoon cinnamon

1/4 teaspoon nutmeg

4 cups fresh blueberries

1 tablespoon lemon juice

Extra sugar for sprinkling on crust

In a large bowl, or the bowl of a food processor, combine your flour, salt, and sugar, either with a whisk or by pulsing a few times. Add in your butter pieces. Using your fingers or a pastry cutter, quickly work the butter into your flour until it begins to look like cornmeal with a few pea-sized butter pieces sprinkled throughout. If using a food processor, pulse for about 10 seconds to get the same effect. Pour your water in a little bit at a time, working it into your dough just until the dough holds together. If using a food processor, slowly pour your water through the feed tube with the machine running just until dough holds together but not for more than 30 seconds.

Working quickly, break dough into 20 golf ball sized pieces. Between two pieces of approximately 8-inch x 8-inch parchment paper, slightly flatten each ball into a disk with the palm of your hand. Put all of the disks in resealable plastic bags and place in the refrigerator for at least an hour, or overnight. Can also be put in freezer for up to 3 months. Pull out of refrigerator 15 minutes before using, or out of freezer 30 minutes before using.

Alternatively, you can skip the golf ball/parchment paper step and simply shape the dough into two equal disks and refrigerate or freeze as above. Then, when ready to use, roll out one disk at a time on a well-floured surface, and cut out 5-inch circles as if making sugar cookies. You'll then use those circles to make your hand pies.

For the egg wash, gently whisk together the egg and water right before baking. Use as directed below.

To make your filling, whisk together your dry ingredients: cornstarch, sugar, salt, lemon zest, cinnamon, and nutmeg. Gently fold in your blueberries and lemon juice.

Preheat oven to 375°F and line two rimmed baking sheets with parchment paper or a non-stick baking mat.

Roll out your golf ball disks to an approximate diameter of 5 inches (or use the 5-inch circles you cut out of the larger pieces of dough).

To assemble the hand pies, spoon 1-2 tablespoons of filling on one side of a dough circle. Using your fingertips or a pastry brush, dampen the edges of the dough with water. Fold the dough over to form a half circle. Pinch the edges of the dough together. Crimp the edges with a fork. Repeat the process until all of the circles are used. Prick each pie on top twice with a fork.

Brush the top of each hand pie with the egg wash and sprinkle generously with the extra sugar.

Refrigerate for 10 minutes. Then bake for 20-25 minutes, or until they are golden brown on top. Let cool a bit before eating. Enjoy!

YIELD: About 20 little pies made with love

THE SIMPLICITY OF A RIVER, A TENT, AND JUST SITTING

The kids had been looking forward to our trip for a year. They had settled into their seats, headphones on, and didn't whine the entire drive. No "Are we almost there?" No "I'm bored." We were headed south on our annual pilgrimage to the Eel River in Northern California.

What is it about the summer road trip and the anticipation of swimming in a river that allows children who can barely sit for half an hour to eat their dinner to sit for nine hours straight in a car without complaining? Their only questions were, "When can we go to the river? Can we go to the river right when we get there? When?"

And sure enough, upon our arrival there was no holding them back. No setting up camp. Just a flurry of bathing suits and sunscreen and they were off.

Maybe the answer lies in its simplicity. In the way that the older kids ferried the younger ones back and forth in a small raft across the deep end all day long. The way they all scaled the big rock up past the poison oak and jumped into the river over and over again. Or maybe it was the thrill of night swimming with only flashlights to illuminate the water. Or the way that the moms — best friends and sisters — still exhausted from the school

year, were allowed to sit. Sit. Sit. Sit. In the sun. Talking about this and that. Sipping sparkling water or a glass of rosé.

At one point, I inquired of ten-year-old Jack in a private moment, "So, are you having fun?"

He replied, "Mom? Are you kidding me? This is my war craft," as he pushed off into the water and kicked his inner tube down the river.

Of course, you can't think of tents and rivers and campfires without thinking of food. Food that's been simplified. Pared down. No cookbooks. No recipes. A loaf of purchased pound cake that someone sliced up and left on a table for children to grab as they walked by for breakfast. A cooler filled with sandwiches for lunch: pb and j, salami and cheese, turkey with hummus and veggies. And for dinner, grilled flank steak with a simple marinade of lime, garlic, and cilantro accompanied by buttered noodles and salad greens tossed with olive oil and lemon juice. Easy. Uncomplicated. No pressure food.

In our tent at bedtime, we snuggled inside sleeping bags, breathed in the night air, and drifted off to sleep. Well, everyone but me with my genetic disposition toward light sleeping; this time, I didn't curse this trait. In the wee hours of the night, I heard the rustle of toilet paper, hushed whispers near the teenage girls' tent, and the shuffling of feet in retreat.

The following day, I explained to my disgruntled teenage daughter while surveying the toilet-papered tent, "Boys do and say these things because they like you."

She replied, "Mom, you always say that."

Just like my parents said it to me.

Back through the redwoods, past the rolling hills of southern Oregon and up to our familiar Douglas fir trees, the only sound in the car was the occasional, "Mom, can we stay longer next year?"

The boys were thinking about what type of water contraption they're bringing next time, my daughter was plotting retaliation, and me, I was reminiscing about the food, that bottle of rosé, and sitting. Just sitting.

GRILLED FLANK STEAK WITH LIME AND CILANTRO

When I was down by the river, my friend, Jill, grilled up a flank steak marinated in a garlic, lime, and cilantro sauce. Wow! As soon as I returned home, I tried to recreate her recipe. I'm not sure if it's exactly the same but it's pretty darn close and it was almost impossible to get a picture of it. I have made it a handful of times in the past month specifically to take a photograph, and it's always gone before I can get the camera aimed. Finally, on the last try, I wised up and took the picture before calling everyone in for dinner.

2 pounds flank steak	*Pinch of red pepper flakes*
1 teaspoon salt	*1/4 cup olive oil*
1/4 teaspoon black pepper	*Juice from 2 limes*
1/2 teaspoon cumin	*4 garlic cloves, peeled and sliced*
1 teaspoon chili powder	*1/4 cup fresh cilantro, chopped*

First, tenderize and score your meat. With a meat tenderizer, gently pound both sides of your steak. Then, using a sharp knife, make diagonal slices about an inch apart across both sides of your meat. Do NOT cut all the way through. Your goal is to make very shallow scratches in the meat to allow the marinade to penetrate better.

In a small dish, mix together your salt, pepper, cumin, chili powder, and red pepper flakes. Rub your spice mixture all over both sides of your flank steak. Next, mix the olive oil, lime juice, garlic, and cilantro in a small bowl. Combine your meat with the marinade in a rectangular shallow dish with a lid or in a resealable plastic bag. Flip the meat over and back a couple times to make sure both sides are completely coated. Stick the meat in your refrigerator and let it marinate for at least 2 hours or overnight, flipping it occasionally.

Take your meat out of the refrigerator 20 minutes before grilling time to allow it to come to room temperature. Pre-heat your barbecue to medium heat.

Pull your meat out of the marinade, slap it down on the grill, close the lid, and let it grill for about 6 minutes. Flip it and grill another 4-6 minutes depending how well done you like it. We here at the Minns house don't like our meat to moo at us while we're eating it, so I usually go for the longer time.

Remove your meat from the grill and let it rest for 5 to 10 minutes, then slice it up and serve. Enjoy.

YIELD: Enough for a family of 5, although if a certain teenage boy happens to stop in for dinner, you may want to grab some shrimp or chicken out of the freezer and put that on the grill as well

CIRCLING ROUND THE TABLE
WITH COWBOY CAVIAR

B*asil, lettuce, rice, peanut butter, shallots, eggs, butter, Parmesan cheese, pasta, parsley, thyme, rosemary, ketchup, oatmeal, raisins, whole grain mustard, sesame oil, vanilla extract, avocados, cherries, black eyed peas, corn, cantaloupe, lime, cilantro, salmon, flatbread, goat cheese, hot dogs, hot dog buns, hummus, salsa, pancake mix, tea, cherry tomatoes, Nana's jam, soy sauce, milk.*

With a pile of cookbooks, notebooks, and recipe cards spread before me, I wrote out the list of groceries that I planned on hauling to the Oregon coast for our two-week vacation. I followed that up with my list of possible dinner menus. The first week we were to be joined by my side of the family, the second week by my hubby's.

First Dinner – App: guacamole, Dinner: grilled salmon with tomato and shallot compote, green salad, rice, green beans, birthday cake for Nana.

Second Dinner – App: Cowboy Caviar, Dinner: marinated flank steak, roasted potatoes, artichokes, bowl of cherries.

I suppose that when most people go on vacation, they spend their planning days laying out activities for their trip. I, on the other hand, think of the food possibilities. The endless options excite me much like a child writing out her Christmas list. The

hope. The anticipation. And the beauty of it is, I'm not alone in this.

In the weeks leading up to this vacation, I received calls from my sister, my mother, my sister-in-law, and my sweetie to talk about food. Who's bringing what? Who's preparing this? Who's ordering out for that? Calls came in from shopping trips to Costco — "Just picked up a bag of those multi-grain chips we like so you don't need to get those." Text messages flew back and forth from the next group coming out to the coast — "@grocery store, need anything?"

Of course, once we were there we participated in all of the usual beach activities: the boogie boarding, the sand castle building, the sand boarding, the dune climbing, the tide pool investigating, the beach combing, the bike riding, the lighthouse visiting, the whale watching, the sunbathing, the book reading, the puzzle making, the game playing, the bonfire building. But during all of this fun, in the back of my mind was always, "When can I start preparing our next meal?"

And once we were all crammed around the table on a various assortment of chairs, we continued to share, not just the meal at hand, but stories about other meals and recipes. An idea on preparing mussels with curry, or marinating steaks with soy sauce and mustard. How to cook clams on the grill. Other ideas for vinaigrettes. Dips for artichokes. Chocolate cakes versus vanilla. We'd ooh and aah over new dishes. The way one family sets up a taco bar that differs from our own way. And I guess what we took away from all of this was inspiration. In sharing our food, our ideas, our recipes with one another, we passed along a bit of ourselves for others to take home with them. The bit that comes directly from our own kitchens, our own homes.

COWBOY CAVIAR

This recipe has circled around my neighborhood dozens of times. I requested it from my neighbor who had it passed along to her by another neighbor. At get-togethers in our neck of the woods, this dip always shows up on an appetizer table. Introduce it into a new group and you will receive emails the following day with requests for the recipe. It couldn't be simpler. It's delicious and it's pretty darn good for you. Obviously tortilla chips are its usual sidekick, but I've been known to scoop it up with sliced red bell peppers or spoon it over toast for breakfast.

1 12- or 15-oz. can black-eyed peas	*1/4 cup olive oil*
1 12- or 15-oz. can corn kernels	*1/4 cup red wine vinegar*
2 avocados, cubed	*2 garlic cloves, peeled and minced*
1/2 cup chopped tomatoes	*1 teaspoon cumin*
2/3 cup cilantro, chopped	*3/4 teaspoon salt*
2/3 cup green onions, chopped	*1/8 teaspoon pepper*

Gently combine all of the ingredients in a medium-sized bowl. If possible, let sit at least half an hour before serving so the flavors have a chance to mingle. Set it out on an appetizer table and watch it disappear. Enjoy.

YIELD: The perfect amount to accompany a bag of tortilla chips

BERRY CRUMBLE
MUFFINS TO SHARE

The whole thing started about eight years ago with a *Welcome to the neighborhood!* jar of pesto. Not a sandwich bag of pesto, or a half-pint jar of pesto, but one of those pickle-sized canning jars filled to the brim with homemade pesto and topped off with a thin layer of olive oil. My new neighbor handed it to me without any pomp and circumstance and said, "I was making some pesto and thought you might like some."

I was moved by her generosity, especially considering that we barely knew each other. I still have that jar even though the pesto is long gone.

Some people are born with the gift of giving. They know how to choose the right thing or the perfect moment to bestow a special something upon another person. I, on the other hand, was not blessed with that gift. The holidays are always fraught with anxiety for me. I never know what to get people. How much to spend. I overthink what they would like. (I still cringe when I think of the batik shorts outfit I gave my sister when she was not three but 23.) Family members, friends, and neighbors around me are natural gift givers, so I can see how it's done. I know how it feels to be the recipient of their generosity and although I want to be a pesto-giver myself, I always talk myself out of all the reasons why someone would like what I have to give.

To my absolute joy over the years, my neighbor did not stop with the pesto. "You have to try this chocolate cake." "A chocolate truffle." "We brought you back some halibut from Alaska." "Thought you might like a homemade vanilla latte." "I brought over these smoked Kokane for you to try along with this rosemary cheddar."

Even her daughter started bringing over gifts: cookies and fancifully decorated cupcakes. And each time, I was as genuinely grateful as the first time and simply enjoyed basking in the glow of gift receivers' delight. That is, until my daughter tossed out the comment, "Mom, we never give them anything." And broke the spell.

I pondered long and hard on Hanna's words. First, I considered the basic truth that I'm not much of a baker. To say, "Here's a few strips of our flank steak left over from dinner" just doesn't have the same ring as, "I brought you a slice of my cranberry chocolate hazelnut tart with homemade caramel sauce drizzled on top."

Second, the overthinking always seems to win out. "They wouldn't want this. Why would they want this? I don't want to bother them. I'm sure I'll be bothering them. They probably don't even like this kind of food. Maybe they have food allergies. I could've made these better. As a matter of fact, these aren't even that good. Actually, these are terrible."

And on and on until I say to myself, "Gads, enough already."

The other day I happened to pop by my neighbor's house for a quick chat and as I turned to go she said, "Oh, I almost forgot…" and disappeared around the corner.

A second later she was back. "We brought you a bag of blueberries from Hood River."

Walking home, cradling my bag of berries, I thought of a muffin recipe I had and knew what I was going to do.

A few hours later, I watched as my daughter headed out the front door to our neighbor's house with the still warm berry crumble muffins. I heard myself say to myself, "Oh, I wish the crumble had more oats. Next time I'm putting more oats in the crumble. Wait a minute…crumble… didn't they say a few years ago they didn't like crumble?"

But as my daughter passed by the kitchen window, I heard my kinder self say, "Enough. Why must you always be so hard on yourself? Let it be what it will be."

That afternoon, my neighbor's daughter was over hanging out and she said to me, "Oh, Carrie, I had one of your berry muffins. It was really good. My mom only let me have one, though. She's making cinnamon gelato right now and she said we're going to have that with the muffins tonight for dessert."

My first thought was one of relief: "Phew, they liked the muffins."

My second thought was, "Where's my share of the cinnamon gelato?"

BERRY CRUMBLE MUFFINS

I must tell you that I had a hard time getting a photo of these muffins for you. Every time I make them they disappear before I can photograph them. I love the mix of blueberries and blackberries, but you can use all blueberries or all blackberries if you prefer.

FOR THE CRUMBLE

1/4 cup light brown sugar, lightly packed

1/4 cup all-purpose flour

1/4 cup old fashioned rolled oats

1 tablespoon flax seed

2 tablespoons butter, softened

FOR THE MUFFINS

1 cup all-purpose flour

1 cup whole wheat pastry flour

2 teaspoons baking powder

1 1/2 teaspoons grated lemon zest

1 teaspoon cinnamon

1/4 teaspoon nutmeg

1/4 teaspoon salt

3/4 cup granulated sugar

1/2 cup butter, softened

2 large eggs, room temp

1/2 cup milk, room temp

1 teaspoon vanilla extract

1 cup blueberries

1 cup blackberries, if extra-large cut in half

1 tablespoon all-purpose flour

Preheat oven to 350°F degrees.

Line your muffin tin with paper liners or grease your muffin cups with butter.
In a small bowl, toss your blueberries and blackberries with 1 tablespoon of flour and set aside.

For the crumble topping, mix together your brown sugar, flour, oats, and flax seed in a bowl. Add your butter and rub it into the flour mix with your fingers until it is evenly distributed. Set aside.

To make your muffin batter, whisk together your flours, baking powder, lemon zest, cinnamon, nutmeg, and salt in a medium bowl. Set aside. In a large mixing bowl, cream together your sugar and butter on medium speed for about 3 minutes.

Scrape down the sides of your bowl. Add in your eggs, one at a time, and mix until incorporated. Stir in your milk and vanilla. Scrape down the sides. Slowly add in your flour mixture just until combined. Do not over mix. The batter will still be a bit lumpy. Gently fold in your berries.

Spoon the batter into your muffin cups, filling only ¾ full. Top each one with a tablespoon or so of crumble mix.

Bake your muffins on the middle rack for 20-25 minutes until golden and a toothpick inserted in the center comes out clean.

Cool in the tin for about 5 minutes. Remove from tin and serve warm, although my family is not picky and will eat them at whatever temperature they happen to be when they discover them sitting on the kitchen counter. Enjoy.

YIELD: About a dozen

FIXING FOOD FOR
JUST THE FIVE OF US

As they circled past our home again, we waved and hollered *good-bye* and *drive safely* with all the fanfare of the first time. I watched as my ten-year-old darted through beach grass and hopped over rocks trying to make it to the next driveway before they did. Trying to make the time with his beloved cousins last a little bit longer. Then my sister-in-law drove around the corner and they were gone.

The week before, when my sister and her little ones left, we performed this same good-bye ritual with the hugs, the waving, the blowing kisses, the circling around a few times. After they had driven out of sight, my five-year-old tapped me on the arm and said, "Mom?"

"What?"

I could see he was trying to keep his lower lip from quivering as he asked me, "When will we see them again?"

Once my sister-in-law's car disappeared, the five of us silently headed back toward the house that moments ago had been teeming with activity and now seemed empty and quiet.

I would be lying if I didn't say that sometimes, during the past couple of weeks with all of the cousins, the noise level and the chaos grew to such heights that I couldn't even hear myself think.

Like a good housewife right out of the 1950, I would holler, "My nerves!" and then proceed to pour myself a chilled glass of Pinot Gris.

But even with that said, I wouldn't change the time we all spent together. And once it was over, each of us was a little wistful that the last of the vacations before school started again was drawing to a close.

That first day of just the five of us, we each retreated to our own corner. Some reading, others listening to music, another dozing in front of the TV. Not sure what to do with the calm. Eventually there were requests for walks to the ice cream store and bike riding along the paths. The next day, we hauled ourselves down to the beach. My older two were out in the ocean. My little guy was quietly, but intensely, building sandcastles, and my sweetie and I were simply sitting. Next to each other. And watching.

In the evening, as I stirred the mixture of garlic and lemon for our shrimp pasta and hummed quietly to Corinne Bailey Ray, I thought about how there was something comforting about the rhythms of my own family. Knowing our likes and our dislikes by heart. The schedule we needed to be on or not. How much activity we needed or how much we could simply be. And even though I had been sad to say good-bye to the cousins, there was something lovely, harmonious even, about being together just the five of us.

(That is until the boys practically broke out into a fistfight over not just LEGOs but LEGO heads. Those teeny, tiny pieces that go on top of LEGO figures and of which we have at least a hundred, but apparently only one of those hundred would do, but hey, the calm was nice while it lasted.)

GARLIC AND LEMON SHRIMP WITH SPAGHETTI

I love this dish. It's fast and can easily be doubled. Perfect for a weeknight. I use fresh shrimp for this in the summer and frozen shrimp in the winter. Often frozen seafood is fresher than the fresh seafood at your grocery store, especially if the seafood was flash frozen soon after being caught. I have made this with bow tie and penne pasta but my favorite is the longer types –- spaghetti, spaghettini, fettuccine, and so forth. And please use fresh Italian parsley for a bit of brightness. It's easy to find in the grocery store (or perhaps your garden) and lasts a long time in your crisper, especially if you wrap it in a paper towel.

1/2 pound spaghetti

1 tablespoon butter

1 tablespoon olive oil

1 pound large shrimp, peeled and deveined (thaw, if frozen)

4 garlic cloves, thinly sliced

1/2 cup reserved pasta water

Juice from 1/2 large lemon

1/4 cup chopped Italian parsley

Salt and pepper, to taste

Grated Parmesan cheese

Bring a large pot of water to a boil. Sprinkle in some salt and drop in your spaghetti. Cook 8-10 minutes or according to directions on the packaging.

Meanwhile, heat a large skillet over medium heat. Add your olive oil and butter and heat until butter is melted. Stir in your garlic and cook for about 1 minute. Add in your shrimp and sauté over medium heat 4-5 minutes or until the shrimp has turned pink all over.

By this time, your pasta should be done. Scoop out ½ cup of the pasta water and set it aside, then drain your pasta.

Once the shrimp has finished cooking, add your ½ cup of reserved pasta water, the lemon juice, parsley, and salt and pepper to taste. Stir gently to combine.

I like to put the pasta in a large pasta bowl and pour the shrimp over the top. Then I gently toss everything together, making sure to coat the spaghetti with the delicious garlicky-lemon sauce. Scoop up into individual bowls and sprinkle with Parmesan cheese. Yum.

Note: If you have an 11-year-old who loves shrimp and he is first in line to dish up, make sure you let him know that he has a 6 shrimp ration. Otherwise, he will take 12 or 15, leaving only a few meager ones to be split between the remaining four members of his family.

YIELD: Serves 4 but in our house, it serves 5 since the kindergartner eats like a bird

SUMMER FRUIT PAVLOVA TO CELEBRATE A MILESTONE

I'm thinking of signing my son up for golf camp, basketball camp, a soccer camp, and maybe some swimming," one of my well-meaning friends said to a group of us about a month ago.

The conversation then led to fall activities. "Besides soccer, we're putting together a flag football team if anyone wants to do it."

I sat there listening, sipping my coffee, and thinking about how different I am now as a parent compared to when my daughter was younger.

She was in swim lessons at six months old. As a toddler, she had a playgroup that met weekly. She was in tumbling classes for years. She could write her name before she entered preschool and ride a bike and tie her shoes before she entered kindergarten.

For my youngest, playgroup and tumbling aren't words in his vocabulary. As for some of the other activities, maybe I had been a bit lackadaisical in teaching my six-year-old those childhood milestones. So I said to my friends, "You know, I think you should count us out. We're still working on, um, some basics."

Later that day, I sat Will down and said, "Guess what we're going to do this summer?"

"What?"

"You are going to have Swim Camp with Mom, Tie-Your-Shoes Camp with Mom, and we're starting with Bike Camp with Mom. How does that sound?"

"Yes!" he replied.

Besides motherly guilt, I felt particularly motivated to get rid of the training wheels because I knew we'd be meeting up with his cousins soon. He would not want to be shown up by his three-year-old cousin who could already ride a two-wheeler.

Day one of bike camp, I called him up from the bowels of our house and out into the driveway. We worked on gliding. I taught him how to use the kickstand, how to use the brakes, and how to start. I held onto the back as he "rode" the bike up and down the driveway. Fortunately, before my back gave out, my neighbor interrupted our training session. She asked me some questions and we chatted for a while.

In the middle of our conversation, I decided to check on Will. As I turned around to look for him, there he was riding his bike out of the garage. On two wheels. By himself. I turned to my neighbor and said, "Sandbagger."

I turned back to Will and shouted, "Woohoo! You're riding your bike by yourself!"

With a huge smile on his face, he stopped the bike, put the kickstand down, took off his helmet, and said to me, "Can I go back in now?"

"But buddy, you just learned to ride your bike. That's so exciting. Don't you want to keep practicing?"

"Well, I was in the middle of a LEGO battle when you called me out here."

We continued our bike camp throughout the week by visiting various parks with tracks, culminating with the park in our neighborhood whose trail travels over bridges, around a pond and up and down hills. He completed the required "two times around the pond" but he really just wanted to play on the playground with some friends who happened to be there.

To celebrate Completion of Bike Camp, I made a special dessert: Summer Fruit Pavlova. As I watched Will enjoy his treat, I thought to myself how different my children are. How my middle guy was the kid who practically taught himself how to ride a two-wheeler at age three. How my eldest could swim as a toddler. And my littlest one, well, he apparently takes on the mantra that my hubby occasionally applies to handyman jobs, "It's not that I can't do it, it's just not how I choose to spend my time."

(Although, let the record state that when the hubs does choose to do handyman jobs, he does a mighty fine job.)

I'll let you know how swimming and shoe-tying go. Let's hope I haven't been spending that extra 20 minutes a day tying and untying his shoes because he can't be bothered to reach down and do it himself.

SUMMER FRUIT PAVLOVA

Usually the pinnacle of my dessert making consists of ice cream with berries or occasionally a pie, but every now and again I get a wild hare to make something different. Since I had a plethora of summer fruit lying around that needed to be used up and pie sounded like too much work, I settled on this Pavlova to celebrate the End of Bike Camp. One thing to note about Pavlova is the meringue base can be made 2-3 days in advance and stored in an airtight container. Once you put the filling and fruit on it, you'll need to serve it fairly soon afterwards or you'll end up with soggy meringue.

FOR THE MERINGUE

4 egg whites at room temperature

1 cup superfine sugar

2 teaspoons cornstarch

1 teaspoon fresh lemon juice

1/2 teaspoon vanilla extract

FOR THE FILLING

1 cup heavy cream

1 tablespoon sugar

4 cups mixed summer fruit such as cherries, peaches, blackberries, blueberries, strawberries, raspberries, nectarines

1 teaspoon lemon juice

Optional: 1 teaspoon sugar

Preheat oven to 250°F. Draw an eight-inch circle on a piece of parchment paper. Flip the paper over so that the pencil marking is on the underside, place it on a cookie sheet, and set aside. In a large mixing bowl and using an electric mixer, beat your egg whites together until foamy. On medium speed, add in your sugar a little bit at a time. Increase your speed to high and continue beating for about 3 minutes or until stiff peaks form. Fold in your cornstarch, lemon juice, and vanilla extract. Stir just until combined.

Spoon your meringue into the circle on your parchment paper. Using the back of your spoon, press down gently in the center to make a shallow well. Bake for about 1 hour to 1 hour 15 minutes or until dry to the touch. With the oven turned off and the door ajar, leave your meringue in the oven to cool completely, up to six hours or overnight.

Shortly before you are ready to serve your dessert, prepare your filling by whipping your heavy cream and 1 tablespoon sugar together until soft peaks form, about 2 minutes.

Gently mix your summer fruit and lemon juice in a large bowl. Add sugar if needed.

When ready to serve, put your meringue on a lovely plate or cake stand. Spoon the filling into the well and top with the summer fruit mix. Put out for your friends and family to ooh and ahh over. Cut into pie slices and enjoy.

YIELD: 6-8 slices

WHEN YOU CAN'T DO IT ALL, DO A TINY BIT

In my backyard are two raised square boxes full of bare dirt. Good dirt. Compost-boosted dirt but still, bare dirt. Not a speck of green except for the occasional weed that chooses to sprout there. Last year those boxes were overflowing with tomato plants, lettuce, and carrots, but this year — nothing.

Blame it on the wettest, coldest spring in 117 years according to local weathercasters, blame it on the kids keeping me so busy it's a wonder I even know my name, or their names, or blame it on the fact that sometimes, no matter how much I might want to, I can't do it all. I'll leave the growing of vegetables to the experts this summer and visit the farmers market more often.

I tell myself that maybe this fall I can get some cool weather plants going in those raised boxes. Probably won't happen. I even suggested to my neighbor that perhaps we could do tandem vegetable plots of cool weather produce. I'll grow the lettuce. She can grow the, um, the turnips and rutabagas. She gave me a polite little laugh. Definitely won't happen.

But despite the fact that I never got around to planting the quintessential summer vegetable garden, I still have my pots of herbs and I have a couple vines that have been giving me unexpected pleasure.

You see, I have this deck, which is so, so hot in the summertime and cold and wind-blasted in the winter. Not many plants can go the distance out there but still I persevere. I look out on that deck every day of my life and darn it all if I'm not going to have something green there. When I explained my dilemma to the helpful gal at my local gardening store, she suggested I plant a pot of beans.

"Eh?" was my first thought.

"You'll have a pot of green all spring, summer, and fall. It won't last through the winter, but the bonus is you'll have the flowers and you'll be able to snack on the beans."

And snack on the beans, I do. I've even gone so far as to whip up some hummus in which to dip those sweet beans. Even my sister-in-law, who was recently in town for a visit, commented on how she'd been out on the deck snacking on the beans while chatting on the phone. Those prolific vines surrounded by oregano, marjoram, and pansies have made it perfectly clear to me that sometimes when you can't do it all, doing a tiny bit is just as pleasurable.

And the best part is that I'm not watering, weeding, fighting pests, pinching back, digging up, or any number of other tasks that go along with growing a vegetable garden. Instead, I'm out on the deck napping (those kids are running me ragged. When does school start?) and having myself a little snack from time to time.

LEMONY HUMMUS

I eat gobs of hummus. So much so that I get tired of buying it and wish for a homemade version. I'm picky about my hummus — it can't be too chunky or too oily, but must be somewhere in between. Inspired by the beans, I finally got up from my nap on the deck and whipped up this smooth version. So easy. Goodness. What took me so long?

4 tablespoons fresh lemon juice (1-2 large lemons)

2 medium garlic cloves, peeled and minced

2/3 cup tahini paste

3 tablespoons olive oil

1-2 teaspoons salt

2 15-oz. cans garbanzo beans (chick-peas), drained and rinsed

3-4 tablespoons water

In a small bowl, stir together your minced garlic cloves and lemon juice. Let stand for 5 minutes. This tames the raw garlic a bit, which I like, but if you are a raw garlic lover you may want to skip the resting period.

In the bowl of a food processor, cream your tahini paste and garlic-lemon juice for about a minute. Add in your olive oil and 1 teaspoon salt. Process another minute. Finally, add your garbanzo beans and process until smooth, about a minute or so. Scrape down the sides from time to time throughout the processing.

Add the water through the feed tube a tablespoon at a time until you've reached your desired smoothness. Dip your finger in the bowl and check to see if the hummus has enough salt for you. If not, add a bit more.

That's it, folks. Dip in your beans, your carrots, your zucchini, your pita chips, or whatever you have. Can be stored in the refrigerator for 3-5 days. Enjoy!

YIELD: About 2 cups

THE SAGA OF THE
TINY PLASTIC BRICKS

I'm a "Go outside and play!" type of mom.

Last March, I was triumphant. After months of organizing and purging, I had moved the mass of LEGO pieces from my upstairs landing and hallway down to the basement. Finally, I could walk to my bedroom without tripping over tiny plastic bits.

I had sorted the pieces by size and type. I had labeled the LEGO drawers. I had a dustpan and whisk that the boys could use to simplify clean up. I had outlined on the carpet with artists' tape each boy's designated building area. I had posted the rules for the new LEGO area.

1. Your creations must stay in your area. If too full, then you must break down old to make way for new.
2. Keep your special guys on your base. If your special guys are in the people drawer, they belong to everyone.
3. Stray pieces must be put away before bed.
4. NO hoarding!

I was elated. I was overjoyed. I laid down on the LEGO-free landing at the top of the stairs, made carpet angels, and reveled in the emptiness of it all.

When people made suggestions of what to put on that stair landing, I panicked. "Nothing. We're putting nothing there. I just want it clear."

When I walked by it, I felt a sense of calm.

I don't know if it was a coincidence of his age, or if it was caused by the migration, but the day the LEGO station went downstairs, 12-year-old Jack, who had spent hours and hours of his life since the age of three constructing intricate creations from plastic bricks, stopped playing with them. On a dime.

My little guy gave the new LEGO area a whirl. He hung in there for a few weeks. But then, while I was busy lying on the clean carpet at the top of the stairs, Will simply infiltrated the living room, the kitchen counter, the kitchen table, the entryway, the window sills, the stair banister, and every surface of his bedroom with tiny LEGO creations. After a few months, he was spilling out of his room into the upstairs hallway and finally, he said to me, "Mom, why can't I just put my base…there?" and pointed to the landing at the top of the stairs.

Last month, upon arriving at my friend Polly's house after an eight-hour road trip, my kids darted for her backyard to jump on the trampoline her kids had received for Christmas. Once inside, they took turns holding the family's new kitten. Hanna looked at me and said, "A trampoline! A kitten! What is your problem, Mom?" insinuating that we have neither and why? Polly looked at me, shrugged her shoulders, and said, "It's just a stage, Care. It's just a stage."

I can still hear her saying that.

I was up early on Friday morning whipping up a smoothie for Hanna who was headed to volleyball practice. I poured in my orange juice, tossed in my banana pieces, some frozen blueberries, a sprinkle of cinnamon, a squeeze of honey, and a handful of ice. I turned on the blender and braced myself for the noise. When the smoothie was finished and the machine turned off, the house went silent.

As I poured the smoothie into glasses, I could hear the faint humming of my little guy and the clinking of tiny plastic bricks coming from the landing at the top of the stairs.

It's just a stage, right?

BLUEBERRY CINNAMON SMOOTHIE

This is my kids' favorite smoothie hands down. (Shouldn't it be hands up? Who came up with hands down?) Sometimes we swap out the frozen blueberries for frozen strawberries or peaches or mangoes but we always come back to the blueberries.

Enjoy!

1 cup orange juice

1 banana, broken into chunks

1 1/2 cups frozen blueberries

A shake of cinnamon

A squeeze of honey (about 1 teaspoon)

A handful of ice (about 1 cup)

Put your ingredients into your blender in the order listed above. I have learned that you want to keep the frozen bits up and away from the blade so the blade doesn't freeze and simply spin instead of blending. Blend until smooth.
Pour into 2 large glasses or 4 medium ones. Drop in a straw. Drink and enjoy!

YIELD: 2-4 servings depending on the glass

TRI-TIP STEAKS WITH CHIMICHURRI SAUCE ON A MUCH-NEEDED WEEKEND AWAY

"Um, Mrs. Minns, I don't think our camp starts until 10:30 a.m.," my 12-year-old's buddy says as I'm minutes away from dropping them at cooking camp.

"Oh no, darling, it starts at 10:00 a.m. I'm sure of it. I have it in my calendar."

It was the first week of summer camps and I had everything timed out perfectly. All three of my chickens needed to be in a different place at a different time, and I was patting myself on the back for having the schedule organized down to the minute.

I pulled into a spot in front of the cooking school. The boys hopped out and headed toward the door, my son's buddy saying under his breath, "I checked the website last night."

We pulled open the door and were greeted by panic in the eyes of the chefs. "Well, hello, there…camp doesn't start for another half an hour, but you are welcome to have a seat over there and wait."

My son's buddy smiled at me and I had to smile back. (Darn these kids and their technological skills.) Clearly, I needed coffee. We found it across the street, and eventually ambled back to the cooking school only to arrive five minutes late.

That is how my summer started and I could never kick out of it.

I would get my daughter to dance rehearsal 30 minutes early twice in a row only to get her to the actual show 30 minutes late.

Thought I had responded to a friend by texting, "Sure I can take your son to lacrosse camp tomorrow. I'll be there by 8:30 a.m." Showed up the next morning and wondered why she had already taken him. Found the pending message later and wacked myself upside the head for never pressing send.

When I drove Jack to register for middle school at the end of August, I couldn't believe the way I had finessed my schedule that day to include volleyball practices, swimming lessons, football practice, my own work, a conference call, and smack dab in the middle of the day, the aforementioned registration. Driving over the speed bumps leading up to the school, I glanced in my rear view window and wondered for a brief moment why there weren't more cars behind us or in front of us.

"Hey, buddy, can you check the calendar on my phone and tell me what time I have down for registration?"

"Noon to one."

"Okay, that's what I thought. We're all good!"

We drove up to the school. Only a handful of cars were in the lot and the doors were shut and locked. Jack started saying things like, "I just wanted to see my friends. I can't believe we missed registration."

"Not to worry. I'll figure this out."

Finding an unlocked side door, we walked in the building and discovered that registration had been from nine to noon.

By the time I got to Labor Day weekend, I was desperate for a break from the constant chore of getting people places on time and failing at it. I was clearly out-numbered by my children and my brain was out of RAM.

We headed to the Oregon Coast for the holiday weekend and like a child, I was antsy the whole ride. I couldn't wait to get there. We parked our car in the driveway and didn't get in it again for three days.

We walked on the beach. Walked to the coffee shop. Rode bikes. Soaked up the rare, hot, Oregon sun. Watched the kids boogie board in the frigid ocean. We read books. Took naps. Watched college football. Caught up with friends. We barbecued tri-tip steaks with chimichurri sauce, ribs with a secret sauce, and oysters on the half-shell with butter. We ate tomato basil salad, cowboy caviar, and sweet cantaloupe. We lit a bonfire. We watched the sunset and chuckled at our teens and tweens roaming the beach in packs. We never had to be anywhere on time.

We weren't there long but when it was time to head home, my mind felt more settled. The franticness had dissipated a bit. "Sometimes you just need a little change of pace," my hubby commented as we were leaving.

Riding home, I felt like I could take on the first day of school the next day, which would include getting three different kids to three different schools.

A week into it, we're not doing too badly. The kids are arriving on time or what we call "Minns time" — 5-10 minutes late — which is perfectly normal for us.

We'll see how long this lasts and when I may need that change of pace again. I suppose my first clue will be when my kids, as well as their friends, start letting me know where I need to be and when.

TRI-TIP STEAKS WITH CILANTRO CHIMICHURRI SAUCE

I mostly disregard food trends. I let the seasons determine what I'm making; however, the recent chimichurri sauce craze would not let me be. Maybe it's the name. I mean, even if you don't have a clue what chimichurri sauce is, don't you want to make it, or at the very least say "chimichurri sauce" three times fast? While the Italians have pesto, and the French have pistou, Argentinians have chimichurri, which they mainly love to drizzle over grilled steak. Traditionally made with parsley and oregano, I've found that the herb combinations are endless. Use whatever you have on hand. You can't go wrong.

One of the beauties of this sauce is that it doesn't have cheese or nuts like pesto, so if you or someone you are cooking for has nut and dairy allergies the chimichurri sauce is every bit as good as pesto. And I find myself drizzling it on just about everything I pull out to eat: prosciutto, goat cheese and arugula sandwiches, tomato and mozzarella slices, hard boiled eggs, avocado, grilled meat and fish, tacos, roasted potatoes, and stirred into quinoa, pasta, or rice salads. This meal brightener will last a few weeks in an airtight container in your fridge.

FOR THE STEAKS

6 tri-tip steaks, 1-inch thick, approx. 2 pounds

Coarse salt

Freshly ground black pepper

¼ cup olive oil

2 tablespoons red wine vinegar

1 teaspoon garlic powder

FOR THE CHIMICHURRI SAUCE

2 cloves garlic, peeled

½ cup parsley and ½ cup cilantro, plus a bit of chives and mint

Or, ½ cup parsley and ½ cup of any combination of herbs: basil, oregano, rosemary, tarragon, chervil

Pinch red pepper flakes

½ teaspoon coarse salt

1 tablespoon red wine vinegar

½ cup Arbequina olive oil or other high quality olive oil

Generously salt and pepper both sides of your steaks. Whisk together olive oil, vinegar, and garlic powder. Combine olive oil mixture and steaks in a resealable plastic bag or other marinating container. Marinate for at least 1 hour, and up to 24 hours.

In a food processor, mince garlic cloves. Add in parsley, cilantro, chives, and mint (or any other combination of herbs), red pepper flakes, salt, and vinegar. Process until herbs are finely chopped. With processor running, drizzle olive oil in through the feed tube. Allow sauce to sit for at least one hour before serving. Sauce can be stored in the fridge for up to a week.

Take steaks out of fridge and stand at room temperature for at least 20 minutes before grilling.

Preheat grill to medium heat. Grill steaks over direct medium heat for about 10-12 minutes for medium rare. Remove steaks from the grill and allow meat to rest at least 5 minutes before thinly slicing against the grain.

Drizzle steaks with chimichurri sauce. Serve and enjoy.

YIELD: Steaks for 6

FRENCH TOAST FOR
LAZY SUMMER MORNINGS

When I was a child I liked to weed. I also liked to deadhead azalea bushes. Sure, the 25 cents an hour my grandmother paid me to do it was nice, but that wasn't my sole motivation. I relished the rhythmic motion of it all — pull one, put it in the bucket, pick one, put it in the bucket. No real thought needed. Just fresh air, immediate proof of my progress, and the opportunity to let my thoughts bounce around wherever they pleased. By the time I finished, my thoughts had settled down into their proper corners and the plot of land or shrub I was working on had been tidied up.

Nowadays, cooking holds that place for me — the cutting, the chopping, the stirring. The opportunity to let my mind wander and, eventually, quiet. Proof of my handiwork in the form of a meal for my kiddos, their friends, my hubby, all of us.

But there are times when no amount of chopping, stirring, picking, and pulling can settle my thoughts. They stay up there buzzing around like static electricity. This happens to me during summer "vacation."

Part of the issue is that my children are out of school. This translates into more noise and more chaos in my house than usual.

The other part of it is my generation's drive to always appear busy, always be productive, always be communicating, always be doing something except what we need most — recharging. Giving ourselves permission to do nothing, and letting our minds have a chance to quiet down so we can actually hear our thoughts.

Because Plan A wasn't feasible — a month in a hammock on some warm tropical island, reading books, no one to care for but myself — I settled on Plan B.

I dubbed our back deck my summer office. Every day at 5 p.m. you will find me out there lounging in a chair, reading a book, sipping some wine, and snacking on a little bowl of pistachios. There I sit and allow myself the chance to just be. To let my thoughts take me wherever they please. There's a bit of reverse psychology at play here. By calling it my office, I create the illusion that I'm actually working, which helps a Type A person like myself be able to justify the downtime.

And you know, there is a calm, rhythmic motion to picking up the wine glass, taking a sip, putting it back down. Pick up a nut, crack it open, pop it in my mouth. Open the book, read a few lines, doze off.

My whole family has been getting into it. I've dragged out tables, twinkly lights, and old umbrellas from the far corners of our attic. Will recently hauled a chair and blanket down from his room. Dave is fantasizing about an entire outdoor couch thing. My daughter would like to add a hot tub and my middle guy, a flat screen TV (not going to happen).

Should you be in the neighborhood around 5 o'clock and would like to try it out for yourself, please, stop by. My sister was recently in town from Seattle for the second weekend in a row simply to sit in the office. We now find ourselves out there for breakfast as well. Just this morning we ate French toast with fresh summer berries in the office. And I don't do breakfast. Before you know it, I'll be hanging a hammock out there to sleep under the stars.

FRENCH TOAST WITH SUMMER BERRIES

When I was growing up, this was one of the dishes in my regular repertoire. When I order French toast in a restaurant or follow someone else's recipe, it usually ends up being too rich for me. Ten-year old Jack and I have the same "rich food radar" and are very particular about how saucy, syrupy, or sugary a dish ends up being. Here's my rendition of the beloved French toast recipe, which was given a big thumbs up by the ten-year old, as well as the rest of my brood. I usually eyeball the ingredients so I've attempted here to put quantities on them, but please feel free to adjust the spices to your liking.

A day (or two) old baguette or challah bread, sliced diagonally, about 12 slices

4 eggs

1/2 cup milk

1 teaspoon vanilla

1 teaspoon sugar

1/2 teaspoon cinnamon

Pinch of nutmeg

2 tablespoons canola or grapeseed oil, at least

Toppings: fresh berries (blackberries, blueberries, raspberries, strawberries, etc.), powdered sugar, pure maple syrup

In a large bowl, whisk together your eggs, milk, and vanilla until well blended. Then, whisk in the sugar, cinnamon, and nutmeg. Set aside.

Put a heavy-bottomed skillet on the stove to warm up. I use my cast iron skillet for this. While it's warming, put 3-4 slices of bread in your mix so they can start to soak up the egg mixture. Turn them over after a minute or so.

With your heat on medium, add your canola oil to your skillet. Once the oil is heated, put your first pieces of soaked bread onto your skillet. They should sizzle a bit. Cook until they develop a nice golden brown color on one side and then flip to the other side. Adjust your heat if necessary. I find that it takes about 2 minutes per side.

While your first batch is cooking, whisk your egg mixture once again and add your next 3-4 slices. Continue with the cooking and soaking until all of your slices are done. You may need to add more canola oil to your skillet as you go along. The hot oil helps give the toast a nice searing.

With your French toast, the toppings, and the plates laid out on the table, call the troops out into your summer office and enjoy.

YIELD: 4-6 servings

Autumn

COLD LUNCH ASSEMBLY
FOR THE MORNING-CHALLENGED

My preschooler has not yet grasped the concept of sleeping in.

In my semi-conscious state, my mind barely registers that he is speaking to me. "Mom?" A little louder, "Mom? What animal sleeps during the day?"

As I try to clear the fog from my mind, I perceive the familiar, soft fur resting against my arm. I pet our 17-year-old feline and reply, "I don't know. Which animal sleeps during the day?"

Will replies back, "Mom. Just think. What do you think?"

"A cat."

Silence. I drift back toward sleep.

"Mom?" A little louder, "Mom? What if there was a slide from heaven to all the way down here? What do you think would happen?"

Snapped out of my dozing again, I reply, "I don't know. What would happen?"

"Mom. Just think. What do you think would happen?"

"I don't know. Granddad could come visit us?"

Silence.

"Mom? Mom? What if a real missile…a real one…got shot in your eye? What would happen then?"

"I don't know."

"Mom, just think. What would happen?"

"If a real missile shot you in the eye, you would die."

Pause.

"What if it just shot you in the arm?"

At this point, I toss off my covers and say to Will, "I don't know. Let's go downstairs."

He follows me saying, "Just think, Mom. What do you think?"

I am not a morning person, although I would love to be one. I have friends who are morning people and I admire how they rise at 5:00 a.m., rattle through emails, and fit in an hour-long yoga class all while I'm still in a deep REM sleep.

Because of this, breakfast is never a grand affair in our home. For all my affinity for food and cooking, if you are a guest in our home you will never be served eggs, bacon, waffles, or sticky buns. Instead, I will point you toward the counter where I have, with great effort, managed to lay out granola, yogurt, and some fruit. Sometimes you will get coffee and sometimes I will direct you to the nearest coffee shop. It takes me a good hour or two to become fully conscious in the morning and unfortunately, it is during those couple of hours that Monday through Friday, nine months of the year, I have the job of assembling school lunches.

As Will toddles down the stairs behind me, I head for the pantry. I grab a tea bag, take a mug from the cupboard, fill it with water from the insta-hot, set the timer for three minutes, and stare out the window. The buzzer brings me back to consciousness. I pull the bag out of the mug, drop in a dollop of honey, stir, sip, and feel the hot liquid make its way down my throat to begin the difficult task of waking me up.

I've realized over the years that because of my impaired mental state in the morning, the lunches must be simple. I am a big fan of sandwiches. I find them to be a well-balanced meal in one tidy package. I do try to vary the type of sandwiches over the course of the year, although, my 10-year-old is happy with peanut butter and jelly every day. So I make sure he gets the best possible peanut butter and jelly sandwich: whole grain bread, organic peanut butter, and Nana's blackberry jam which we look forward to receiving every Christmas. Today, however, I decide to mix it up a bit.

I heave the cutting board onto the counter, walk two feet to the refrigerator, open the door, and stare. With the door held wide open (as I've instructed the children not to do), I try to remember what it is I need. Oh, yes. Cream cheese.

Goat cheese. Pesto. I grab an heirloom tomato from the bowl on the counter and go to work assembling the sandwiches. I spread a layer of cream cheese on my 10-year-old's sliced baguette and goat cheese on my daughter's and then a slathering of pesto on both. Thick slices of tomatoes, at the peak of their harvest, come next. I place the other half of the baguette on top of the creation, and plop the sandwiches into their respective lunch boxes. I include some sliced peaches, a piece of dark mint chocolate, and a water bottle, and place the lunchboxes by the door. I holler to each child that it's time to go, kiss the tops of their heads and send them out the door with a "Have a great day! I love you."

I close the front door and turn back into the suddenly silent house. Fully awake and energized, I can now begin my day. Walking to the kitchen, it dawns on me that a little person remains in the house. A little person who has been sitting on the couch, through the entire morning frenzy, patiently waiting. Then, as if we were still back upstairs snuggled under the covers and hadn't just sent everyone out the door, he says to me, "But, Mom. What would happen if a real missile shot your arm? What do you think would happen?"

HEIRLOOM TOMATO SANDWICH

Sometimes the best recipes are the simplest. This one falls in that category, but the secret is to use the best possible ingredients you can find. I do not recommend this recipe in January but only in late summer and early fall when tomatoes have celebrity status at the farmers market. You can go hog wild and make your own pesto for this, but oftentimes I find homemade-quality pesto at my grocery store or farmers market.

One baguette
Goat cheese or cream cheese, softened
Basil pesto
2-3 heirloom tomatoes, thickly sliced
Salt and pepper

Slice your baguette horizontally and then vertically into 3 or 4 sandwich-sized pieces. Slather a layer of goat cheese or cream cheese on the bottom halves. Next, spread a layer of pesto. Lay tomato slices on top. Sprinkle with salt and pepper. Cover the scrumptious filling with the other halves of the baguette. With a napkin handy, bite down on the heavenly creation. Share the other sandwiches, or not. Enjoy.

YIELD: 3-4 sandwiches depending on how big you like them

PARENTING CROSS-EXAMINED

"How do you know when you should be your child's advocate? Or when their hurt is nothing more than a lesson from life? Do you have a conversation with that teacher? That parent? That coach? Or do you stand back and let life take its course? Life's not fair. We don't always get what we want, even if we play by the rules. Were past generations of parents wiser for knowing how to stand back and not get involved? Or will our children be better for having us stand up for what they deserve?"

These questions run through my mind as I jam my hoe-like tool into our god-forsaken clay dirt. I am planting bulbs — those shallot look-alikes that must be planted before the clay earth is morphed into brick by frigid winter temperatures. I do not enjoy planting bulbs, but plant I do. I have 150 of these guys to get in the ground. Years ago, I instituted a rule to prevent over-zealous bulb buying. "You may not buy more than 25 bulbs at a time. You must plant those 25 bulbs before you buy any more." Clearly, I'm not abiding by my own rules.

The questions continue to run through my mind as I dig. "If I choose to have a conversation, will it be perceived as petty? Another over-involved parent? Or appreciated for what it is… communicating? Trying to come to an understanding? And at what point do I hand over the torch and let them be their own advocates with me cheering them on? When are they old enough to do that? And if they don't step up, maybe the true desire wasn't there for them, only me. Does my child feel slighted? Or do I?"

We don't get much of a spring here in the Pacific Northwest. Actually, we don't get a spring at all. We go from cold, gray, and rainy in the winter to cold, gray, and rainy in the spring. The only sign that spring has actually sprung is the myriad of daffodils that beam their cheerful yellow trumpets along roadways, lining fences, and clustered near front doors. They make me smile on gray spring days, which makes the effort to get them in the ground worth it.

I prod the earth while the questions continue to circle. "How do we separate what we want for our children and what they want for themselves? What do they truly have the talent for and what is just wishful thinking? What do they truly love to do and what do we love them to do?"

I pull out my shovel to slip in the bulb as the earth tumbles back into my newly dug hole. Arrgh. I grab a trowel and try to dig faster than gravity. Is my hole three times the height of the bulb? When I glance at the pile of bulbs still waiting to be planted, I decide that this hole is good enough and plant the bulb. We'll see what happens come spring.

I answer my string of questions with maybes. "Maybe we can never know the right answer. Maybe we make the best decisions that we can as parents and that's good enough. Then we wait and see what happens."

The sky is beginning to darken. I grab a whiff of a neighbor's dinner and my stomach growls. I gather my tools and my basket of bulbs. I leave them in the garage and head inside to chop up some actual shallots for our dinner. My work out here is done for now. Tomorrow, I'll begin again.

STRING BEANS AND CARAMELIZED SHALLOTS

This time of year, I serve these string beans on a weeknight with a roasted chicken I pick up at my grocery store and boiled fingerling potatoes tossed with olive oil, apple cider vinegar, salt, and pepper. Like French fries, it's always good to toss an extra pinch of salt on the beans right before serving.

1 pound haricots verts (string green beans), stems removed

2 tablespoons olive oil

1 tablespoon butter

2 large shallots, chopped (about 1 cup)

½ teaspoon kosher salt

Freshly ground black pepper, to taste

Blanch your string beans in a large pot of boiling water for 1-2 minutes (3-4 minutes if your beans are fairly thick). Drain immediately and spray them with cold water to stop the cooking process.

Heat your oil and butter in a large sauté pan. Add your shallots and sauté on medium low to low heat for 10 to 15 minutes, stirring occasionally, until translucent and golden. If your shallots seem to be browning too quickly, turn your heat down a bit.

When your shallots are done, add your drained green beans to the pan, along with the salt and pepper. Heat only until the beans are hot. Don't even bother with forks and knives. Eat these with your fingers. Enjoy!

YIELD: Enough for a family of 5

THE LEGEND OF THE HIDE-BEHIND MONSTER

My evening started out as pure bliss. I sipped wine and munched on appetizers with two dear friends. Our children played in my friend's house and we were left alone to chat. We talked about the kids' new teachers, books we had recently read, and the story circulating that there was a bobcat afoot in our neighborhood. He had reportedly been seen sunning himself on the side of the road, peeking through the rails of back decks, and even chasing a female runner up a wooded trail. "Apparently," my friend told us, "he's not easy to spot due to his coloring, but the telltale sign that he's nearby is the frenzied chirping of the birds."

While we were deep in conversation about what we would do if confronted by the bobcat, our hostess laid out her version of pizza: thick slices of heirloom tomatoes covered with caramelized onions, Herbes de Provence, chopped pecans, and crumbled blue cheese.

As I inhaled my "pizza", I told my friends that I've always been nervous to walk alone. When I was growing up my father regaled my siblings and me with the Legend of the Hide-Behind Monster. No one ever sees the hide-behind monster, he said, because no matter how quickly you turn your head, he is always behind you. What's more, he's a tricky monster,

because he doesn't show up in mirrors. My father would remind us, especially when camping, "Be listening, kids. You know the hide-behind monster is around when you hear the crack of a tree branch and two hoots of an owl."

I said to my friends, "Throughout my childhood, I always carried the feeling that someone was behind me. I would dart up dark stairwells as quickly as possible. Then I would twist around, trying to catch a glimpse of whoever was there. Nobody ever was. So now I not only need to worry about the imaginary monster from my childhood but an actual bobcat as well?"

When the sky grew dark, I reluctantly packed up my little tribe and headed home. We had received notice that our street was to be slurried the following day (which meant nothing to me except that I wanted to start singing "Surry with the Fringe on Top") and all cars needed to be off the street by 8:00 a.m. Being morning-challenged, I knew I should take care of my car that night. I dropped the children at home and parked the car on the next street over. A five-minute walk through a trail in the woods connects our two streets. Easy, right?

I parked alongside the cars of others who'd had the same idea and headed down the trail toward home, armed with a flashlight that beamed a quarter-sized circle of light.

All was going well. I was talking to myself about the pizza, humming Rogers and Hammerstein show tunes, and shining my little pin of light. But as I went down into the darkness, the ferns flanking the sides seemed to grow above my head. I could barely make out the trail. The darkness was swallowing me up, pressing on me, suffocating me. I was alone in the pitch black. I started to take deep breaths, switched to whistling "Whenever I Feel Afraid" and pulled out my cell phone, hoping to gain a little more light by shining it on the ground. And then I had the feeling that someone or something was behind me. Certain I was about to be attacked, I flipped around. I heard the crack of a tree branch, the frantic chirping of birds, and an owl hooting. My heart started racing and so did I. I ran across the bridge, and started to fly up the stairs on the other side. I was on the verge of screaming, "Help!" convinced that the bobcat, a person, or the hide-behind monster was about to grab me, when my feet lost their footing on the gravel stairs. I slipped and fell down. Hard.

Stunned, with a throbbing elbow and skinned knees, I lay there. The light from my neighbor's front porch shone on me through the ferns. I prayed that neither she nor anyone in her family had been peering in this direction the minute before. I shook my head, slowly stood up, and chastised myself. "Look at you. A grown woman. You really need to get over it. The hide-behind monster does not exist!"

I methodically climbed the final stairs, turned the key in my front door, and went into my sleeping house. As for the bobcat, who knows?

TOMATO, BLUE CHEESE, AND CARAMELIZED ONION PIZZAS

This recipe was inspired by the pizza creation of my friend, Julie Lee, who is a master of the appetizer table. The herb, nut, and cheese combinations for these "pizzas" are endless. Basil, almonds, and goat cheese would be delicious, as would cilantro, pistachios, and queso blanco. I serve these to my children, who inhale them. I put the blue cheese and nuts on the side and let the children decide if they want to load up on all the goods or not. These pizzas are also a thoughtful touch on the appetizer table for friends and family avoiding gluten.

2 tablespoons olive oil

1 tablespoon butter

1 large or 2 medium onions, peeled and thinly sliced, Walla Walla or Hermiston Sweets

3-4 heirloom tomatoes, sliced ½ inch thick

1/2 cup crumbled blue cheese such as Rogue River Blue

1/3 cup chopped, roasted pecans*

1 teaspoon Herbes de Provence or 2 tablespoons of a variety of chopped, fresh herbs such as basil, thyme, oregano, and a pinch of rosemary

Salt and pepper to taste

Heat/melt your olive oil and butter in a large skillet over medium heat. Add your onions to your heated fat, stir them around to coat them in the mixture, and then turn your heat down to low. Add a pinch of salt and pepper. Don't be frugal with your onions. Trust me. It's better to have more than you can ever imagine, because they will cook down. Way down. Keep your heat on medium low to low and stir the onions from time to time. After about 20 minutes, they will become translucent and take on an amber color. Take care not to let them brown too quickly or burn, which will give them a bitter taste.

To assemble your pizzas, put a forkful of your caramelized onions on each tomato slice. Next, sprinkle the blue cheese over the onions, then the pecans, and finally the herbs and salt and pepper to taste. Serve them up to your friends and watch them swoon.

*To roast your pecans, spread them out in a single layer on a cookie sheet. Roast for 10 minutes, stirring halfway, at 350°F.

YIELD: About 12 pizzas

LESSONS LEARNED FROM
THE TOOTH FAIRY TRADITION

In our household, we find the tooth fairy to be a flighty little thing who is picky, picky, picky. After surviving another round of the molting process, my children will wrap their precious gift in a tissue, seal it in an envelope, and place it under their pillows to await her arrival. More often than not, come morning, their little eyes will be filled with tears instead of joy. The tooth fairy did not come.

Just as disappointed as they are, I shrug and say, "Maybe she doesn't do envelopes anymore. That's what I did, but maybe now she prefers the box."

"What box?"

"You know. The special little box that holds teeth?"

So, into the box the wee bit of ivory goes. Come morning, there are times when they find she even snubs the box. To my children's questioning gaze, I sigh before exclaiming, "Ah ha! Maybe you just have to leave it out in plain view. Otherwise she can't…she can't sniff it out. Her sniffer isn't working."

While the location for the exchange of goods is unreliable, the tooth fairy is consistent in her payment for a molar: a Susan B. Anthony gold coin. However, as my child races down the stairs to show me her reward, I brace myself. When she opens her sweaty palm to show me the warm coin, I have to force myself not to recoil away from that face. The stern Susan B. Anthony face that seems to say to me, "What are you doing to further my cause? My life's work for women's rights?"

I quickly fold up the child's hand, pat her on the head and say, "Good job. Now why don't you go put that somewhere safe."

I often wonder what I'm actually doing to further the cause of women put in motion over a hundred years ago. My feelings swing between the elation of being alive at this point in history, when women enjoy freedoms not even conceivable a century ago, and the despondency I feel when I hear the latest tragedy suffered by women somewhere in the world. And when that feeling of *What can I, one person, possibly do?* rises up in my throat, I turn on Pink Martini, pour myself a glass of cab, and start chopping. Something. Anything. Today it's the herbs gone wild in my garden's last push of the season that I'm using to liven up an herbed goat cheese spread.

My chopping tool is a perfectly sharpened chef's knife. It's the prized possession of my 10-year-old son, Jack, and perhaps the sole reason he did not complain the entire week of summer cooking camp. He knew that for a week's worth of work, he would come home

with the king of cooking tools. The tool for which, using his birthday money, he purchased a locking case and had to really think about whether it would be okay for me to borrow it occasionally.

Perhaps furthering the cause of women is less about how I raise my daughter and more about how I raise my sons. Perhaps. Perhaps, not.

If I can teach my sons to nourish themselves, to appreciate the preparation of a meal, to gaze out at their yard and recognize it as the support system from which they too can harvest herbs, tomatoes, carrots, and lettuce, then maybe, just maybe, they will treat the earth a little more tenderly. Maybe they will be a little more deliberate when deciding what to put in their mouths. They might know the feeling of satisfaction that comes from making and sharing a meal, of nourishing themselves, their families, and the women who surround them.

I must admit that not much cooking has gone on since the completion of his camp but occasionally, like today, he'll see me chopping and say, "Hey, Mom. Do you want me to do that?" After I pass the knife over, he'll instruct me by saying, "Now, Mom, you're really supposed to hold the knife like this. See?" I'll try not to smile and simply be grateful that a tiny seed has been planted. I don't know if it will grow, but I'm glad it's there. And maybe the next time I see Susan B. Anthony's face, I'll realize that it's not a look of disappointment, but the simple fact that nobody smiled in pictures back then.

HERBED GOAT CHEESE SPREAD

I make this spread year-round with whatever fresh herbs are available in my garden. In winter, I use rosemary. In summer, I love to use basil and in fall, it's the thyme that runneth over my rock walls. Of course, you could use any medley of your favorite herbs. My daughter and my youngest love this and are always thrilled to find it set out on the table along with some flatbread crackers, dry salami, and cucumber slices. Sometimes I toss cherry tomatoes with olive oil and basil and pile them up on toasted bread spread with this goat cheese. Other times, I do the same with fresh peach slices and basil. My three-year-old nephew will inhale an entire eight ounce portion of this spread if left alone with the bowl. Needless to say, it's a winner, unless, of course, you don't like goat cheese.

2 tablespoons olive oil

2 medium garlic cloves, peeled and thinly sliced

1 tablespoon fresh herbs, chopped: rosemary, basil, chives, oregano, thyme, or any combination of these

8-oz. plain goat cheese, softened

In a small saucepan, heat your olive oil over medium-low heat. Turn your heat to very low, add your garlic, and sauté 1 minute or until the garlic is soft and fragrant but not brown, stirring often. Remove from heat. If I use rosemary, I usually add in a sprig with the garlic cloves and let it simmer. The rosemary flavor is mellower this way rather than adding chopped bits of it to the goat cheese. Once the garlic has finished cooking, remove the garlic (and the rosemary if using) from the oil with a fork and discard. Set aside the oil and allow to cool to room temperature.

Put your goat cheese in a medium bowl. Stir in 1-2 tablespoons of the garlic-infused olive oil. I usually add in 1 tablespoon, taste it, and then add more if I desire. Add in your fresh herbs and gently stir to combine.

Spoon the delicious spread into a lovely bowl. Top with a few sprigs of the herb you used. Voilà! An appetizer to impress. (Although I've been known to eat it out of the container, standing at the counter, with no one to impress but myself and it's still good.) Enjoy.

YIELD: A small bowl of herbed goat cheese spread

ALL IS SAFE AND SOUND CHICKEN

The warm smells from dinner lingered in our house — smells from a tender beef stew, or chicken and dumplings, or my mother's chicken and wild rice soup with her homemade dill bread. The dishwasher hummed and the voices from the TV were distant as I made my way down the long, darkened hallway toward the single glowing lamp above the piano. I sat down on the bench, sighed, and pushed up the lid to reveal the keys. I opened my book and searched for Mr. Burke's purposeful handwriting that marked the current week's assignment. As I reluctantly placed the correct song against the stand, my father quietly slipped into the living room and took up his place in his favorite chair. With his feet up, his hands clasped over his chest, and his eyes closed, he said to me, "I love listening to you play, Sweetie Pie."

And there he sat while I banged out songs like "Candy Man" and "You're a Grand Old Flag" or the occasional "Für Elise." He sat there during the weeks when I threw myself down on the bench in tears claiming, "I will not practice the piano tonight!" He waited as I pulled myself together, wiped the tears, and began again with the "Blue Danube."

Now, when I look back, I'm so grateful for those practice sessions — the smells, the darkness, the hushed tones, my father's presence, and the sound of the piano. I felt safe. Even knowing that my father would most likely be leaving soon to stand guard again on a naval aircraft carrier in some far-flung ocean…still, I felt safe.

That same piano sits in the living room of my home. The one my mother was determined her children would play. The one that my parents had to carry over a swinging bridge and up a winding path to get home. The one with the salamander burned into the wood just behind the stand.

In deep fall, when the kitchen has been put away and the baby has been put to bed, I'll pass that piano and something will pull me over to it. Possibly the lingering smells from our dinner of chicken sautéed with garlic and tomatoes, the early darkness of the evening, or knowing that the eldest children are in their rooms reading and for a minute, no one needs me. I will flick on the lamp, pull out the bench, put up the familiar music, and start to play. My out-of-practice fingers will trip over themselves at first. But soon, they will remember the way and I will play song after song — from "Winter Peace" to "Thanksgiving" to "Jessica's Theme." I will play, I will be lost in the music, and I will feel safe.

Then whether it be a sixth sense or mother's intuition, I will feel a presence with me while I play. Something will cause me to stop and look. There in the semi-darkness of the stairwell, I will see my eldest children peering through the railings and listening. And further back in the darkness of the kitchen, I will just make out my hubby smiling at me.

CHICKEN WITH SHALLOTS, GARLIC, AND TOMATOES

In our household, I'm a bit of a short order cook based on the type of chicken people like. Some want dark meat, some want white. Whatever mix of pieces you use, make sure they are bone-in, skin-on. The meat will be much more flavorful and tender than boneless-skinless and you can always pick off the skin once it is cooked. I like to serve this with couscous or quinoa, which soaks up the delicious sauce from the pot. Don't let it go to waste, as my mom would say. It's heavenly.

8 bone-in, skin-on chicken thighs, or 4 thighs and 2 bone-in, skin-on chicken breasts, or a similar mix

2 tablespoons olive oil

1 tablespoon butter

3 large shallots, peeled and coarsely chopped

4 garlic cloves, peeled and sliced lengthwise

1 15-oz. can diced tomatoes

4 sprigs fresh thyme, leaves removed, stems discarded, or a couple pinches of dried thyme

Salt and pepper, to taste

Begin by seasoning your chicken pieces with salt and pepper. Next, heat/melt the olive oil and butter in a large heavy-bottomed pot. Add the chicken pieces to the pot and cook them on all sides over medium heat until they are lightly browned. Add the shallots and the garlic and lightly brown them for a few minutes, but do not let them burn.

Next, add to the pot your tomatoes, thyme, a couple pinches of salt, and a pinch of pepper. Cover the pot, reduce heat to medium-low to low, and cook for 15-20 minutes or until the meat is cooked through. Enjoy the aroma that will linger in your home the night through.

YIELD: 4-6 servings depending on size of appetites

THE NEWLY APPOINTED
SECRET KEEPER

I'm not ashamed to admit that when the ten-year-old's football coach suggested we get his wrist checked out, my first thought was not the welfare of my child, but the fact that this checking out would occur on one of my rare free days. Those precious days during the week when all the chickens had flown the coop and the house was silent. Could his wrist really be that bad? I knew he had been cradling it in the palm of his other hand like a fragile bird for two days, but come on, did it truly warrant a trip to the doctor's office? Which would then result in a trip to the radiologist? Which would take up the whole day?

I picked him up from school mid-morning and we headed down the windy road toward town. He was giddy — like he'd just drawn a "Get Out of School FREE" card. After checking in at the doctor's office, we tried to quarantine ourselves in the corner of the waiting room, wishing we'd brought facemasks to guard against the swine flu virus floating around the room. Jack asked me, "Do I have to go back to school after this?"

"If this is it, yes. If you end up getting x-rays, no. There won't be enough time."

As we made our way out of the building with his x-ray slip in hand, I could tell that Jack was resisting the urge to skip.

After the x-rays were successfully taken, we still had a bit of time before we needed to head home. Which was perfect, because I had something I'd been wanting to talk with Jack about. Now was the right time. I suggested, "Let's go up to Pittock Mansion and take a quick look around. It's such a beautiful day. The mountains are probably out and you can name all of the bridges for me." (Being able to identify each of Portland's ten bridges is quite the badge of honor for elementary school kids in this city.)

As we walked around the grounds, taking in the late fall beauty and looking at Mt. Hood in the distance, I draped my arm around his shoulders and said, "So, I've been wanting to talk to you about something. Something really serious. Something I can finally talk to you about now that you're ten."

I could see him tense and the gears of his mind work backwards as I went on. "I heard you and your sister talking the other day about Santa Claus. About how you know it's…us."

He immediately fired back with, "What? Mom? Awww. I don't want you to tell me that."

"But," I said, "I heard you two talking. You know. I heard you say you figured it out because Dad bought something at

Target when you were with him and then it showed up under the tree 'From Santa'."

"Yeah, I know, but I don't want you to tell me."

"Well, sweetie, now that you know, I need to talk to you about it. You have a very important job to do now that you know the truth."

"What?"

"You need to keep the secret. You cannot ruin it for your little brother. When he's your age he will figure it out on his own but for now, you have to keep the secret going."

There was no lack of the older brother taunting the younger brother with his superior intellectual knowledge and I didn't want the secret of all secrets to be the fall-out victim in this show of superiority. We continued to chat about it. About comments his friends had made regarding the jolly old man. About the importance of honoring the younger sibling's right to be young. And about other clues that had led to his discovery.

"Like last year, there was a 50% off tag on my General Grievous LEGO® set from Santa."

We had finished circling the gardens at the mansion. It was time to be heading home. Jack seemed satisfied with our chat, satisfied to know that he had an important job to do as keeper of the secret.

On the way home, I realized I had failed to take him on the requisite after-the-doctor's-office trip to the ice cream store, so I did a mental inventory of ingredients I had at home that would fill this oversight. When we got home, I got to work.

An hour later, I laid his fresh-from-the-oven apple tartelette down in front of him. He slowly looked up at me with one of those pensive, furrowed brow looks and said, "So Mom?"

He paused a brief second, and then came out with it. "So Mom, who's the Easter Bunny?"

APPLE TARTELETTES

Eating one of these tartelettes — warm buttery crust, tender apples, and a sweet caramel-like sauce — is like pulling on wool socks, a cozy sweater, and curling up with a cat. I think I ate half of the tartelettes myself from the last batch I made. They really are best eaten soon after they come out of the oven with tea, coffee, or vanilla ice cream. If they last another day, pop the stragglers in your toaster oven or regular oven at 350°F for a few minutes to bring back the crispness of the crust. These tartelettes are equally delicious made with pears.

1 sheet puff pastry, thawed

2 medium baking apples, peeled, cored, and sliced (Honeycrisp, McIntosh, Granny Smith), about 4 cups

Juice from ¼ lemon, about 1 teaspoon

3 tablespoons butter

1/4 cup brown sugar

1 teaspoon cinnamon

Pinch or two of nutmeg

1 egg, lightly beaten

Small bowl of water

Turbinado/coarse sugar

To start, pull your puff pastry sheet out of your freezer and set it on a plate on your counter to defrost for 20-30 minutes. Preheat your oven to 350°F. Line two cookie sheets with parchment paper or silicone baking mats.

Peel and core your apples. Cut them into approximately ¼-inch thick slices. Put apples in a medium bowl. Sprinkle lemon juice over them, gently mix, and set aside.

In a high-sided skillet, melt butter over med-low heat. Whisk in your brown sugar, cinnamon, and nutmeg, and stir until all is combined. Pour your apples into the butter/sugar/spice mixture and gently toss to coat evenly. Remove from heat and set aside.

On a lightly floured surface, roll out your puff pastry to approximately 15 inches x 15 inches. Cut into 9 5x5 squares. Doesn't have to be exact — squares, rectangles, it all tastes good.

Place squares of dough on prepared cookie sheets. Lay about 6 apple slices on each square leaving 1/4 inch around the edges. With your fingertips, dab a little water around the edges, then roll the edges over and pinch the corners. Drizzle each tartelette with extra sauce from the pan if you'd like. Brush the rolled edges with the egg. Sprinkle with a bit of turbinado sugar for sparkle.

Bake for 20-25 minutes, or until edges are lightly browned and apples are just tender. Enjoy, my friends!

YIELD: 9 tartelettes

PEAS AND PANCETTA ON THE NIGHTS I'M WORN DOWN

The week started out with Will, the preschooler, trying to make use of his limited vocabulary. In a moment of peak frustration he hollered at his brother, "Just…just…just go put your head in the potty!" and stormed out of the kitchen.

Older brother Jack shrugged his shoulders and muttered, "Good dis, pal. Real good dis."

This is how the week began and it never kicked out of its irritating mood. Every day was like an itch you can't reach in the middle of your back.

The following morning, Hanna flew down the stairs wearing a masterpiece of middle school fashion. She had only minutes to spare if she was going to make the bus. I sized up the ensemble that surely took hours to put together and before I could stop my textbook reaction, I said, "Wait a minute, sweetie. You can't wear that to school. Your skirt is too short."

She looked at me aghast and replied, "But Mom, everyone wears their skirts like this."

"Well, not you. Go change and make it quick."

On Thursday, forty-eight hours before tricks and treats, I was in the middle of the costume store and had to remind Jack that no, I wasn't kidding when I told him he couldn't get the mask with the blood pumping through it because I found something inherently wrong with it. To which he said, "But Mom, all my friends have that mask. It's so cool."

"Well, I guess you'll have to be something original."

And by the end of the week, I wondered if I was stuck in a never-ending groundhog's day because every time I consciously took stock of how I was spending my time, I found myself in the car. "Here I am driving. Here I am, still driving. Wasn't I just driving? Gads, I'm gripping this steering wheel again. Somebody help me, I'm driving again. I'm driving again and the same song is playing on the radio every time I'm in here. Arrgh…somebody save me from this car!"

I found myself wanting to pull over to the side of the road, yank out the radio, and chuck it into the bushes.

Then without warning, I came upon it — a little bit of frozen time where the road behind me slipped beyond the bend and the road in front of me was hidden by the horizon. All the aggravation of masks and skirts and heads in potties disappeared. My attention was captured by the sunlight filtering through the fall leaves and the branches arching over the road. I felt as if I were slipping through an arbor leading somewhere magical.

And for that instant, I was able to clear a tiny spot in my mind. A spot that reminded me to breathe, to slow down over the speed bumps, and that peas and pancetta are good on a night when I am worn down and out of patience.

Then as quickly as I came upon it, the magic was gone and my mind filled back up with the scratchy humming of life.

PEAS AND PANCETTA WITH BOWTIE PASTA

This is one of our favorite go-to meals. It's quick to make and I almost always have a bag of peas in the freezer and pasta in the pantry. If I don't have pancetta, I substitute a package of bacon. Oh darn, bacon.

4 cups frozen petite peas	*1/2 teaspoon freshly ground black pepper*
1 tablespoon olive oil	*1 pound dried bowtie (farfalle) pasta*
1/3 pound pancetta, diced	*1 cup pasta water*
2 large shallots, peeled and diced	*More salt and pepper, to taste*
1 teaspoon salt	*Freshly grated Parmesan cheese*

In a deep sauté pan with a lid, cook your frozen peas in boiling water until tender, about 3 minutes. Drain them in a colander and spray with cold water to stop the cooking.

In the same sauté pan, heat your olive oil, add in your pancetta, and cook over medium heat, stirring occasionally, until golden brown and crisp-edged, about 6 to 8 minutes. Reduce your heat to medium-low, add in your shallots and cook another 3 to 4 minutes, stirring occasionally.

Meanwhile, fill a large pasta pot with water, a pinch or two of salt, and bring to a boil. Add in your pasta. Cook your pasta according to directions on package.

Before you drain your cooked pasta, reserve 1 cup of the pasta water. Pour ½ cup of the pasta water as well as the cooked peas into the sauté pan with the pancetta and shallots. Heat mixture over low heat, gently tossing together. Stir, taste, and add more pasta water, salt, and pepper, if needed.

Serve over bowtie pasta with freshly grated Parmesan cheese on top. Enjoy!

PS: If you forget to reserve the pasta water, never fear. Just add some water, or a little chicken broth if you have some hanging out in the fridge or don't add anything and it will be delicious all the same.

YIELD: Enough for a family of 5 with a bit leftover. Perfect for a thermos in a lunchbox the next day.

ACKNOWLEDGING THAT
AUTUMN HAS TRULY ARRIVED

"No. I don't want you. Get back in your closet. I don't care if you used to be my favorite. I'm not ready for you!" I wailed last week.

With a sigh, I said good-bye to the sun and braced myself for seven straight days of wind and rain as forecasted by my weather page. Autumn has always been my most cherished season of the year. But not this time. Maybe it's because our summer here in the Northwest didn't really start until the beginning of August. Maybe it's because due to the ages of my children, we can actually have fun on our summer vacations nowadays. Maybe it's because I was still hoping those little green peppers were going to grow bigger and turn red. Maybe it's because it took me longer than usual to recover from the previous school year and hence, I wasn't prepared for this school year to start. And since I was still not recovered from the previous school year, how was I possibly going to get through the impending holiday season? Whatever the problem, I was not ready to usher in my favorite season of the year.

But autumn was here whether I was ready for it or not. I tried to drum up some seasonal spirit by putting a sprinkling of fall decor around the house and a string of lights on the front porch. I spent an afternoon raking the leaves off my front lawn and breathed in that cool, crisp air.

I turned on the heat and pulled out my favorite pink wool sweater to wear in the evenings. After school one day, to the delight of my children, I set down mugs of hot apple cider topped with a dollop of whipped cream and a sprinkle of cinnamon. Saturday morning found me huddled under umbrellas with my mother and father. We hooted and hollered as my 11-year-old and his football team fought their way into the playoffs. You could say I was going through the motions to embrace the season. But it was after the football game, during a seemingly non-moment, that I found myself unable to resist autumn's charms.

There, sprinkled on the deck of a grocery store parking lot, was a kaleidoscope of color. Leaves in all shades of crimson. And the sheer beauty of those leaves lying there in the rain against the stark contrast of the pavement made me catch my breath.

Smiling, I hopped into the car and drove up through the fog toward home. Into the kitchen I went. Bowls and mixers made all kinds of racket and Vince Guaraldi floated out of the speakers. My sweetie passed through and casually asked, "Do you ever stop producing?" I was too focused on baking a loaf of pumpkin bread with chocolate chips to reply. It was time to properly welcome in autumn.

Now here I sit, after the frenzy of a long weekend and the baking extravaganza, warm in my favorite wool sweater. A cup of tea and a plate of crumbs from the slice of pumpkin bread I had for breakfast sit next to me. A sick child is upstairs. My voter's pamphlet is in front of me. All thoughts of going back to bed have long since been silenced. Out the window, brilliant reds and yellows play out against a backdrop of creamy white fog and I think, "Okay, okay, I'm glad you're here."

CHOCOLATE CHIP PUMPKIN BREAD

As I mentioned above, I had a hankering to make pumpkin bread over the weekend. I combed the internet high and low, pulled out cookbook after cookbook, searching for the perfect pumpkin bread recipe, but every recipe I found called for at least 3 CUPS of sugar, if not more. I just couldn't, in my right mind, add 3 cups of sugar to a single loaf of bread. So I put on my alchemist hat and set out to create my own recipe. I found my results to be rather delicious, especially still warm from the oven. A few days later, the flavors had mellowed and mingled, giving the bread an even richer flavor.

1 cup all-purpose flour

1/2 cup whole wheat pastry flour

1 1/2 teaspoons ground cinnamon

1 teaspoon ground ginger

1/2 teaspoon ground nutmeg

1/4 teaspoon ground cloves

1 teaspoon baking soda

1/4 teaspoon baking powder

1 teaspoon salt

1/3 cup milk

1 teaspoon vanilla

6 tablespoons unsalted butter, softened

3/4 cup granulated sugar

1/4 cup brown sugar

2 large eggs

1 cup pumpkin puree

1/2 cup dark chocolate chips

Bring out all of your refrigerated ingredients so they can warm to room temperature. Next, position a rack in the middle of your oven and preheat to 350°F. Grease a 9×5 inch loaf pan.

In a medium bowl, whisk together your flour, cinnamon, ginger, nutmeg, cloves, baking soda, baking powder, and salt. Set aside.

In a small bowl, combine your milk and vanilla. Set aside.

In a large bowl, beat your butter until creamy, about 30 seconds. Gradually add in your sugar and beat for 3-4 minutes. Next, beat in your eggs, one at a time. Add your pumpkin puree and beat on low speed just until blended.

Add the flour mixture in three parts, alternating with the milk mixture in two parts, beating on low speed or stirring with a rubber spatula until smooth and scraping the sides of the bowl as necessary. Fold in your chocolate chips.

Pour into your prepared loaf pan and bake for 60 minutes or until a toothpick inserted into the center comes out clean. Let your loaf cool on a rack for 5-10 minutes before taking out of the pan and allowing to cool completely. Enjoy.

YIELD: One fragrant loaf

AT THE HEART
OF OUR HUMANITY

I chuckled to myself as I typed my message and sent it out to all 43 of my Twitter followers, "Left home 4a. Arrived San Francisco 8a. BlogHer Food starts tomorrow. Had coffee. Now what?"

I looked up to see if anyone noticed what I had just done. I glanced over at the man playing the violin on the bench next to me, at the daddies doting on their tiny baby, and at the still-locked front door to Miette Bakery. No one seemed to be aware of my virtual ramblings. In my uncharted territory of social media, this was how I learned — by pressing buttons, sending things out, and seeing what came back.

Bare minutes passed before a tweet appeared for me. "Come hang out with Katie and me." I was giddy. It was like finding an extra-large piece of chocolate in my bowl of dark cherry, chocolate, and vanilla ice cream.

I hadn't been the new kid on the block for a long time. My hubby and I had managed to stay put for eight years. Growing up, however, I was always the new kid. This was due in part to my father's military career, in part to constantly changing school boundaries, and in part to my parents' incessant need to move from one house to another every three years (18 moves and counting for them). Once again, though, I was a new kid with

a ticket to the sold-out BlogHer Food Conference in San Francisco and I didn't know a soul. However, Kristen Doyle, who writes the blog Dine and Dish, and I had spent the past year admiring each other's photographs online. We had never met in person but we had a developed a virtual friendship. It was Kristen who replied to my Twitter message.

Somehow I managed to hail down a cab in the sleepy Hayes Street neighborhood in which I had enjoyed my coffee and hightailed it to my hotel. I was thrilled to learn at the reception desk that my room was ready this early in the morning. I turned around to head for the elevator and found Kristen waiting in line behind me. She looked just like her online profile picture. From that moment on, she brought me into the fold and I am eternally grateful.

The days and evenings that followed were a whirlwind. I sipped Beringer wine and chatted with the Deen brothers. I heard Dorie Greenspan speak of her years working with Julia Child and tasted the creamy, almost velvety, tomato soup prepared by Portland's own Chef Lisa Schroeder of Mother's Bistro. We took midnight Muni rides, went on a scavenger hunt at The Ferry Building, and dined on crispy bacon dipped in chocolate.

But it was the people I met from all corners of our country, with the accents to prove it, who made the biggest impression on me. I felt a connection amongst strangers who have a strong commitment to food and I believed the connection existed out of concern. Most of us shared the knowledge that we, as a society, were sick. We had lost our way with food. We could no longer find our way around a kitchen. We no longer brought people into our homes to share food. The amount of inspirational speaking I heard that weekend was extraordinary, but the closing remarks by Michael Ruhlman left us all speechless. At the end of his talk, the emotion of what he had to say was so great, he stood and paced the stage. "Cooking is what made us human. Cooking made us more social. We had to cooperate and divide labor. We had to come together. I think you all write about this because in your heart you know cooking is fundamental to our humanity."

Humanity, as defined by Webster's: "All human beings collectively. The quality of being humane; kindness; benevolence."

Sunday morning was a bit like the end of summer camp. Ready to go home but sad to leave my budding friendships, I hopped into a cab with two others bound for the airport. During the ride, I met Ahmed and his son who had been in town visiting family. We exchanged pleasantries. Ahmed asked me what I did and the name of my website. Without a shred of an accent, Ahmed shared that he was raised in Egypt, "the birthplace of civilization" and then went on to tell me that French was his first language.

"Perfect," I thought. "Beware thee that choose to entitle their website with a French phrase. Thou shalt be quizzed by native French speakers in French."

And quiz me he did...in French. I suppose I passed when he said to me in French, that from now on when people ask me if I speak French, not to say in French, "I can speak French, but it isn't pretty." But to say, "I do speak French but with a petite American accent." Kindness prevailed in him not to call it a grand accent.

However, it was the final English words he spoke that resonated so strongly with me. Before departing the cab, he turned to me and said with great earnestness, "Language is our culture. Food is our humanity."

He held up his hand as if to wordlessly cut-off any argument, paid for my cab fare, and then he and his son hopped out and disappeared. In the suddenly quiet cab headed for my terminal, I was left to ponder language and food. Kindness and humanity.

CREAMY TOMATO SOUP

I'm not even going to try and pass this off as Chef Lisa's tomato soup. To enjoy her exquisite concoction you'll have to visit her restaurant, Mother's Bistro in Portland, or buy her cookbook, Mother's Best. *But this is what I serve my family when I don't have a lot of time and want something homemade. I accompany it with toasted cheese sandwiches and sliced apples on the side. If you are really short on time you could bag the toasted cheese sandwiches and put out some bread, a hunk of cheese, and a knife, and tell everyone to go at it. I usually double the recipe, as it's perfect in a thermos for lunch the next day. You can also freeze it, if you are a freezing food kind of person.*

1 large onion diced (a cup or so)	*1/2 teaspoon salt*
2 tablespoons olive oil	*1/8 to 1/4 teaspoon cayenne pepper*
2 28-oz. cans diced tomatoes	*1/4 cup sour cream*
2 cups chicken broth	*Grated sharp cheddar cheese*

In a heavy-bottomed skillet, heat your olive oil. Add your diced onions and sauté for 8-10 minutes, or until onions are softened and translucent.

Add in your tomatoes (plus their juices), chicken broth, salt, and cayenne pepper. Bring to a boil. Then reduce heat and let simmer, uncovered, for about 20 minutes.

At this point I usually pull out my 18-year-old hand-held immersion blender and purée my soup a bit. If I'm running short on time, I don't do this and just leave it fairly rustic. It's up to you. However, if you don't have an immersion blender, you must go and get yourself one, especially if you're like me and have a phobia about cleaning food processors except in extreme situations.

Once that is done, whisk in your sour cream until creamy. Spoon into bowls and top with the grated cheese. Enjoy!

YIELD: A big pot full

PUMPKIN PIE TO MARK SOME FIRSTS AND SOME LASTS

Just three weeks ago, I dropped my littlest one off for his first day of kindergarten. I'm still not sure how I feel about it. A little happy. A little sad. While his older sister is always representative of firsts, Will represents lasts. Last diaper. Last binky. Last sippy cup. Last one to entertain all day. Last one to curl up on my lap. Last one to be at home with me. Last one to hold my hand.

"How was your first day of kindergarten?" I had asked him when I picked him up.

"Good," he replied.

"And what did you do?"

He responded, "I did recess and PE." Then he let go of my hand and ran off hollering, "Can I play on the playground before we go home?" He was taking the whole thing in stride, not knowing that this first for him was a monumental last for me.

A month into kindergarten, I walked Will and Jack home from school — Jack led the way and Will dawdled behind him. As Will scrambled to catch up, he slipped ever so slightly on the gravel while his backpack, almost half his size, swung from side to side. He turned back to me and hollered, "Mom! Mom! I have a treasure for you." In his tightly closed fist, he held four dandelions, all in various stages of blooming. He gallantly presented them to me, smiled, and ran off to catch up with his older brother.

A little further up the trail, he stopped again — a twig, a heart shaped stone, a three-leaf clover, a stem of Queen Anne's Lace. "Do you like when I give you treasures, Mom?" he asked, this littlest one of mine.

"I love when you give me treasures."

And then having asked hundreds of times before and already knowing the answer, the same answer I gave his brother before him, he asked again, "What do you do with the treasures?"

"I tuck them in my pocket to keep them safe and when I'm missing you, I pull one out and think of you."

He smiled again, pleased with his good deed, and ran off in search of more tiny treasures.

At home, with backpacks stowed beneath the bench and lunch boxes emptied, I placed a slice of pumpkin pie and a mug of warm chocolate milk down for each boy — our annual fall ritual. I like to mark the beginning of October, the celebration of fall, and the countdown to the holidays with pumpkin pie. I prefer to eat pumpkin pie when it can truly be savored and not shoved in after a long, heavy meal.

I got up to clear my plate and felt my throat catch as I glimpsed the Queen Anne's Lace hanging out of my pocket. A myriad of lasts started to flood my mind — last pumpkin pie to mark the kindergarten year, last one to ask me to come closer so he can whisper in my ear, last one to throw stones in the stream wishing for his kitty to come back — but then I shook my head and told myself, "Don't do this. Concentrate on the firsts."

First one to go to kindergarten without tears. First one to make his own breakfast before the age of 10. First one to organize his own social life before junior high. First one to know that if the LEGO® store or Santa doesn't have it, eBay will. First one whose first day of kindergarten marked my first day to reacquaint myself with myself since beginning this parenting trip with his sister 13 years earlier. Who am I now? What will I do now that all of my children are in school full-time? Where will this new chapter in my life take me? And that first is kind of exciting.

CLASSIC PUMPKIN PIE

You probably have a go-to recipe for pumpkin pie, but on the off chance that you don't, keep this one handy for the upcoming holidays, or keep it handy to make a pie just because. Every Thanksgiving, my daughter is in charge of pumpkin pie and a few years ago, she and I did a pie bake-off to try out different crusts — all butter, all shortening, half butter / half shortening — and we decided that the all-butter was the blue ribbon winner. You can make it in advance, which means less time in the kitchen on any of the big holidays. The filling recipe is one my friend Karna passed on to me, and I tinkered with it to arrive at the recipe I use today.

FOR THE DOUGH

2 1/2 cups all-purpose flour

1 teaspoon coarse salt

1 teaspoon granulated sugar

1 cup (2 sticks) chilled unsalted butter, cut into large diced pieces

1/4 to 1/2 cup ice water

FOR THE FILLING

3 eggs

3/4 cup sugar

1 can (15-oz.) pumpkin

1/2 teaspoon salt

1 teaspoon cinnamon (heaping)

1/2 teaspoon nutmeg

1/4 teaspoon ginger

1/4 teaspoon cloves

1 can (12-oz.) evaporated milk

In a large bowl, or the bowl of a food processor, combine your flour, salt, and sugar, either with a whisk or by pulsing a few times. Add in your butter pieces. Using your fingers or a pastry cutter, quickly work your butter into your flour until it begins to look like cornmeal with a few pea-sized butter pieces sprinkled throughout. If using a food processor, pulse for about 10 seconds to get the same effect. Pour your water in a little bit at a time, working it into your dough just until the dough holds together. If using a food processor, slowly pour your water through the feed tube with the machine running just until dough holds together but not for more than 30 seconds.

Working quickly, pour your dough out onto a lightly floured work surface and gather it into a large ball. Divide dough in half and flatten each half into a rounded disk. Wrap in plastic wrap or parchment paper and place in the refrigerator for an hour before using. You can also put the dough in an airtight bag or container and put it in the freezer for up to 3 months. Pull out of refrigerator 15 minutes before using, or out of freezer 30 minutes before using.

When you are ready to bake your pie, preheat your oven to 450°F.

On a lightly floured surface, roll out your dough to about 12 to 13 inches in diameter and 1/8 inch thick or so. Gently place it on your pie plate. Using kitchen scissors, trim the dough so it hangs over the edge about ½ inch. Tuck that extra dough under the dough around the rim. Then using your thumb and pointer finger on one hand and your thumb on the other, push those fingers toward each other, crimping the dough, around the entire circumference. Pop your prepared dough in the fridge while you mix your filling.

Beat the eggs, sugar, pumpkin, and spices together. Then blend in your milk. Pour your mixture into your waiting pie shell and carefully ease it in to the middle rack of your oven. I always put a cookie sheet on the rack beneath the pie to catch spills.

Bake at 450°F for 10 minutes and then at 350°F for 50 minutes or until a toothpick inserted in the middle comes out clean.

Allow pie to cool completely before serving. I prefer to eat my pumpkin pie with a scoop of vanilla ice cream. I also tend to serve this to my kids for breakfast, after school, and right before bed. Enjoy.

YIELD: One pie

A SIMPLE DISH WITH
A REGAL AIR

Maybe it's that the days are shorter, the kids are in bed earlier, the house is quieter, and the rainy season has begun. I don't know. But on the occasions when the afternoon sun bursts through our windows and lays down a warm path of light across our floor, I look for that furry feline.

A month into our marriage, my hubs and I were still in the stage where we were more than happy to appease each other's obsessions — me pretending to be a runner and him pretending to love furry little animals. Somehow knowing that this stage wouldn't last forever, I dragged my new spouse across town to a cat lady's house and pulled down off the curtains a feisty young feline, which we would bring home and have with us for the next 18 years. (As for the running, I quickly dropped the ruse.) To foster bonding between man and beast, I encouraged my husband to name our bundle of joy. He pronounced him "Bruce." And Bruce it was. Others came after him — another cat, an 80-pound dog — but at the 18-year mark, Bruce was the only one still around.

He had this way of silently being everywhere, as if he could materialize out of thin air. You would sit down and there he'd be, curled up on your lap or trying his darndest to snuggle up on your chest and nestle his head in the crook of your neck, which could be a bit awkward for guests. One minute you were sure you were alone, and the next minute he was eerily sitting ramrod tall right next to your keyboard while you typed. Every now and then, he'd step on the keyboard just to make sure you noticed him. And the lawn…it never looked better than when he moonlighted as a mole catcher and left proof of his handiwork on the front porch.

I tend to put out of my mind the fact that he could actually fling poo and that he found it necessary to cough up a hairball wherever we would least suspect it but were most likely to step in it. He was known to howl like a coyote for hours, especially in the middle of the night when he didn't get his way. (That howl saved his life when, in his old age, he lost his way home.) During a full moon, he would run from one end of the house to the other like he'd sniffed too much catnip. And he had a peculiar tic of sucking his paw that could be thought of as tender and sweet or just plain weird, depending on your mood.

A couple of nights ago, as I prepared our family dinner of herbed chicken simmered in wine and served along roasted potatoes, I looked for him. I expected him to be silently standing nearby, regally sniffing the air around him like some upper crust feline while secretly hoping that one small morsel of chicken might fall to the floor. But he wasn't there.

Don't you think it's true that whether it's a person or a hairball-coughing cat, when they are gone, we don't think of the good or the bad but simply their presence? We miss their warmth and the comfort of their being? And I definitely miss that howling, paw-sucking, poo-flinging, furry feline.

Bruce went to the Happy Hunting Grounds in April where I'm sure he is happily keeping the lush grounds mole free. It's strange, though, how I miss him most now. Now that the house is quieter.

OREGANO CHICKEN WITH LEMON AND WHITE WINE

Now that Thanksgiving is but a few hops away, I'm assuming most of you have planned out the main feast, but what about the other nights? This is a dish I love to serve to guests. (Be forewarned, drinking the wine that you'll be cooking with while you're cooking can lead to lots of animated chatting and loud laughing which will ensure that the dinner won't actually hit the table until 8 p.m. or later.) This dish has only a few ingredients, minimal prep, and sits in the oven for 45 minutes. I use a variety of white-meat and dark-meat chicken pieces with the bone-in and skin-on. This makes for moist meat and you can always take off the skin once it's done cooking if you'd prefer not to eat it. For a gluten free version, simply omit the flour and the dredging. As a testimonial to this dish, the last time I made it my five-year-old said to me, "Mawm, you prob'ly won't be too surprised when I say this to you, but that dinner was so delicious!"

A medley of skin-on, bone-in chicken pieces, about 3½ to 4 pounds

Kosher salt

Freshly ground black pepper

¾ cup all-purpose flour

3 tablespoons olive oil

1 cup dry white wine (I usually use a Pinot Gris)

4-6 sprigs fresh oregano leaves (stems removed and discarded), about ¼ cup of leaves

3 bay leaves

Juice of ½ lemon, about 2-3 tablespoons

1½ cups water

Preheat your oven to 425°F.

Generously sprinkle your chicken pieces with salt and pepper. Put your flour on a plate and dredge your chicken pieces through it, coating them evenly and shaking off the excess.

Heat your olive oil over medium heat in a Dutch oven — a heavy-bottomed pot with a lid that can move from stove to oven. Add your chicken pieces, skin side down, and cook for 5 minutes. Flip your pieces over taking care not to tear the skin.

Slowly and carefully pour in your white wine, lemon juice, oregano, and bay leaves. Simmer and allow wine to reduce for about 2 minutes.

Pour in 1½ cups of water, put the lid on your pot, and put the whole concoction in the oven for about 45 minutes.

If you are using breasts, check them at 35 minutes. Juices should run clear or internal temperature should be 165°F. They may be done since they cook more quickly than the dark meat. If so, remove them, tent them with foil, and continue cooking the remaining pieces.

I usually cut into quarters one pound new potatoes — fingerling, red potatoes, etc. — toss them with one to two tablespoons olive oil, a few pinches of salt and pepper, and a few sprigs of rosemary, lay them on a roasting sheet, and put them in the oven along with the chicken when there is about 25-30 minutes left of cooking time.

When the timer goes off, take the lid off your pot and allow the skin to crisp for another 5 minutes.

Put your chicken on a platter. Remove and discard the bay leaves from the pot. Pop a ladle next to the pot and have people spoon the heavenly au jus over their chicken and potatoes.

If you don't want to monkey around with preparing the potatoes, you could serve this with rice or pasta which would also soak up all of the au jus beautifully. Enjoy!

YIELD: 5-6 servings

THE PERFECT MEAL AT THE END OF A LONG RIDE DOWN THE HIGHWAY

On a highway in the middle of Mt. Hood National Forest, our car was in park and the engine off. Even though there was an unending line of cars behind us in the same predicament, it was strangely quiet. Dark. The snow was gently falling all around us — those big feather-like flakes. We were headed to Sunriver in Central Oregon, which was our yearly Thanksgiving destination. Nana and Papa, aunts and uncles, and a gaggle of cousins were awaiting our arrival. But here we were, stopped on this oft-traveled highway. A highway I'd traveled my entire life. A highway that felt like an old-time movie to me.

I thought about how almost ten years ago I had been parked here as well, facing the other direction. My 11-year-old was a baby and we had just rung in the 2000 New Year. I was in a panic about whether to take him out of his car seat to nurse him because I was never sure when the line of cars would start moving again. To entertain his sister, I sang nursery songs for the hours we were parked on the highway, because that was back when I thought children should not have electronic devices in the car but instead should gaze longingly out the window and let their imaginations run wild. But that was then. Now, I looked back at my three children,

lit up by the glow of the movie they were watching with headphones on in the quiet, quiet car, and I thought, "Thank goodness I came to my senses."

As the line of cars started moving again, little bits of memory from my life flickered by in my mind as we made our way down the road. The spot I handed off the baton during my one and only Hood to Coast relay race. The little church in which I sang "One Hand, One Heart" at the bride's request. (Poor thing should have had me stick to just playing the piano.) The end of the Glade trail in Government Camp — our back door way to get off the mountain from all-night New Year's Eve skiing. The turn-off for Timothy Lake where we survived the Dust Bowl '03 camping trip, which rendered our children so covered in dirt, they looked like extras from the set of *Grapes of Wrath*.

A few hours later, a few more miles down the road, we stopped again. I was under the car dealing with chains and cursing myself for not taking the forecast for snow more seriously. My hands were covered in grease. I thought of the times when as a teenager I had to put chains on our Toyota and how often I had put them on the wrong tires: front instead of back. Or was it back instead of front? Not far from here was the road marker I somehow backed into and blew out the back window of our car in 100-degree weather. Not sure what to do about it in the middle of nowhere, I kept driving while the cat howled and my eldest children, preschoolers at the time, cried. My sweetie still raises an eyebrow at me no matter how many times I say to him, "Cross my heart, hope to die, I never saw a road marker."

Moving again, we passed the turn-off for the shortcut into Maupin where I had hit a rabbit at one in the morning while driving my '73 VW Beetle on the way to the meeting spot for our white water rafting trip on the Deschutes River. Back when my sweetie and I were newlyweds and we road tripped in the middle of the night. I was still sad about that rabbit. On and on down the road we went, and on and on played the grainy film of my life.

A week later, the ten-hour drive and Thanksgiving behind us, we struck out onto the highway again headed for home. This time we opted for the more southern pass but the same grainy movie played as we drove: Sipping a latte at Sisters Coffee Company last summer. Camping under the stars and fly-fishing in Camp Sherman back in college. Driving a golf cart around Black Butte Ranch as a teenager. Wondering if that rope swing stills hangs on the edge of Suttle Lake all these years later?

I felt as if I were in an old silent movie house as these little scenes played out. Only the sound of the film clicking as it went round and round the reel could be heard. It made me think that this is how life works. We keep driving down the highway and life happens. Scenes are filmed.

The snow gave way to rain signaling that we were almost home. We pulled into our driveway just in time for me to make dinner. It took me a while to shake the feeling that I'd just left a dark movie house and stepped out into bright light. The film wound down and the clicks came more and more slowly as I pulled ingredients from the pantry to whip up a quick Tomato and Red Pepper soup. By the time I set the bowls down, sprinkled with grated cheddar cheese, tortilla chips, and cilantro, the movie was over. I was back to creating new scenes. Scenes that would eventually be spliced into the film of my life when it played out again on some long, snowy drive down a highway.

ROASTED RED PEPPER AND TOMATO MEXICAN SOUP

My sister passed on this recipe to me and I love how easy it is, as well as delicious. It's a great one to keep handy as you're getting ready for the holidays and don't have much time to cook. The salsa you use can really change the flavor of this soup. The last time I made this soup, I used a tub of fresh medium salsa I found in the back of my fridge, but a jarred salsa works equally well. I served it with some homemade guacamole and sliced pears because that's what I had in the house, but you could also whip up a little green salad or just serve it as is.

2 tablespoons olive oil

1 yellow onion, peeled and diced

4 cloves garlic, peeled and minced

2 boxes (32-oz. each) roasted red pepper and tomato soup

1 cup corn, frozen or canned

2 cups salsa

2 cups cooked* chicken breasts, cut into bite-size pieces OR 1 large can of white chicken meat

Possible toppings: grated cheddar cheese, tortilla chips, sour cream, chopped cilantro, hot sauce

Heat your olive oil in a heavy-bottomed soup pot. Add your onions and sauté for about 8-10 minutes, or until your onions soften and start to become translucent. Add your garlic and sauté one minute more. Pour in your roasted red pepper and tomato soup. Add your corn, salsa, and chicken. Bring to a boil. Then turn down the heat and simmer for 10-15 minutes. Ladle into bowls and top with cheese, chips, and cilantro. Enjoy.

*The last time I made this soup, I poached a couple of boneless, skinless breasts to use in it. I sprinkled my chicken with salt and pepper and put it in a small pan. I covered it with some chicken stock that I needed to use up, but you could use water or a combo of the two. I sprinkled in a teaspoon or so of Herbes de Provence, tossed in a bay leaf, put the lid on, and brought it to a boil. Then I lowered the heat and let it simmer with the lid on for 15 minutes. The chicken cooked while I put together the rest of the soup. The timing came out perfectly.

YIELD: One big pot full

WHY I LOVE SIX-YEAR-OLDS WHO LOVE A RUSTIC PEAR GALETTE

Why do I love six-year-olds? Well, for one, they still skip. They hum. They hold your hand when they cross the street. When they spy you on the hill waiting for them after school, they run to you as if you are the most important person on earth. When they get to you, they give you a big, gummy, fang-like smile with scabby lips. While walking home they tell you things like, "Justin said he has a billion, trillion LEGO® sets. I think he's lying."

They ask you strings of questions like, "How is the sun made? Is it like a match? Is it two space rocks rubbing together? What does heaven look like? Have people seen it? Is Bruce kitty up there? What eats a bobcat? Can anyone be more than 100? What about 1000? Hey, Mom, what's a thousand minus thirty-one?"

Their whole world has been opened because they are now reading and they take it very seriously — almost as seriously as reciting the names of every Clone Commander in Star Wars. They still believe in Santa but are starting to ask, "Why can't Santa bring me both the Republic Ship and the Death Star?" When they find a joke* that gets a reaction such as, "How do you divide ten apples between eleven people?" they tell it over and over and over again. And when they are tired of walking home in the rain, they simply squat down. They will not budge until they are good and ready.

They still sit down and have afternoon snack with you, whether it's pretzels and a handful of raisins or a slice of Rustic Pear Galette – a new recipe their mom was trying out which proved to be a winner. They will still curl up in your lap for a hug and let you sniff their sweet heads. Not for long, but they'll do it. They leave you love notes that say things like, "yr the Best mom eve. I love you mor then ene wun in the hoe wid worod."

In the early evening while their mom is playing the piano trying to relax, they will quietly assemble a custom LEGO creation for her, complete with a piano, pulled-back hair, a little lamp, and a cup of tea. They are always calling out your name in the house because "I just want to know where you are."

And quite honestly and maybe most importantly, six-year-olds help take the edge off the fact that their older sister has one foot out the door.

You remember when she used to do all of these six-year-old things, but it's gone so fast. You hardly see her anymore. And some days you feel like you've been reduced to her personal chauffeur. But then she'll surprise you. She'll come up behind you, all 5 foot 8 inches of her, drape her arms around your shoulders and say, "Hi, Mom…."

And you'll reach up to touch her arms and say, "Hi, babe…" and you'll be thinking, "Oh, good, she's still here."

A RUSTIC PEAR GALETTE

My, oh, my, if you try out one new pastry-type dessert this fall, let it be this Pear Galette. My fam loved it so much I almost didn't get a photo of it because it disappeared right after the shutter snapped. The hubs even left me a little sticky note next to the empty pie plate that said, "Wow!"

2 cups all-purpose flour

1 tablespoon granulated sugar

1/2 teaspoon salt

3/4 cup unsalted butter, chilled and cut into cubes

3-4 tablespoons ice water

4 firm-ripe Bartlett pears

1/4 cup dark brown sugar, firmly packed

1 teaspoon vanilla extract

1/4 teaspoon ground cinnamon

1/4 teaspoon ground nutmeg

Pinch of salt

Optional: egg wash: 1 egg white lightly beaten with 1 tablespoon water

Turbinado/coarse sugar

Start by making your dough. No, no, don't go buy store-bought. You can do this. So easy. Put your flour, salt, and sugar in a large bowl, or the bowl of a food processor. Whisk or pulse a couple times to combine.

Using your fingers or a pastry cutter, quickly work the butter into your flour until it begins to look like cornmeal with a few pea-sized butter pieces sprinkled throughout. If using a food processor, pulse for about 10 seconds to get the same effect. Pour your water in a tablespoon at a time, working it into your dough just until the dough holds together. If using a food processor, slowly pour your water through the feed tube with the machine running just until dough holds together, but not for more than 30 seconds.

Turn the dough out onto a lightly floured surface and gently knead it until it all comes together in a ball. Slightly flatten the ball into a disk. Wrap in parchment paper, put in an airtight bag, and refrigerate for at least 30 minutes.

While the dough is chilling, preheat your oven to 350°F and take care of those luscious pears. Peel them, core them, and cut them into thick slices. In a large bowl, using a rubber spatula, gently combine your pears with the brown sugar, vanilla, cinnamon, nutmeg, and salt.

Line a baking sheet with parchment paper.

Take your dough out of the refrigerator and roll it out on a lightly floured surface until it's about a 14-inch circle. Carefully lift it and set it onto the parchment paper on your cookie sheet. Arrange your pears over the dough, leaving about a 2-inch border. You can toss out any juices that accumulated in the bowl. Gently fold the dough over the edge of the pear filling. There is no right way to do this, which is why it is rustic. If you want your dough to have a finished look, brush the edges of the dough with the egg wash and sprinkle lightly with sugar.

Carefully slide the whole concoction onto a rack in the middle of your oven. Bake until the crust is a beautiful golden brown, the pears are soft, and your whole house smells like fall, about 50 minutes.

If you can wait, let it cool a bit. Then slice it into wedges and let your friends and family eat it like a piece of pizza...only better. Enjoy.

You make applesauce.

YIELD: One fragrant pear galette that will disappear in milliseconds

BEAN AND CHEESE QUESADILLAS
FOR BALANCE

I closed up my summer office and made it through the first full week of kids back in school, coupled with all their activities. And this past weekend, I was beat.

Before the weekend even started I told my daughter, "I will only drop you off and pick you up one evening this weekend, not both, so choose wisely." She scrounged up rides to the other places she wanted to go, but without a full understanding of why I couldn't just take her.

And I remember when I didn't fully understand. When I paced the sidewalk and was aghast that my mother was late to pick me up from volleyball practice. Or when I'd pick at the dinner she kindly made me and think, "I don't feel like this," even though I'd been asked numerous times earlier what I felt like for dinner. Or when she would write a check in the grocery store line or stop for gas on the way home and I'd feel my heart race with impatience.

I find it horrifying that I even had those thoughts. To admit that I was so impatient and unable to see past my own needs, but I suppose all children act this way at one time or another. At least, that is what I remind myself when I get a similar reaction from my children as to why I cannot pick them up one more evening in a row at 11 p.m. from across town, or why I cannot drop everything and take them to the mall / lacrosse field / toy store that instant, or why we are having bean and cheese quesadillas for the second night in a row, or why I have to quickly stop at the grocery store on the way home.

I notice their sighs, their rolled eyes, their impatience, but curiously it doesn't rile me. They have no way of knowing how much work it takes to be a parent. They won't know until they have children of their own. I shrug it off and simply say to them, "I'm only one person."

And so, here at the start of the school year, I remind myself that I am a mother, yes, a wife, yes, but I'm also a woman with goals and ambitions that lie outside of my family roles. I try to guard my time. Become almost selfish about it as I strive to find the right balance between all of the directions I'm pulled. And yet, I'm still only one person. Not always finding balance…but trying.

To my children, I usually follow up the "I'm only one person" line with "Help me out here, people. There are three of you and one of me. I'm just tryin' my best." And really, isn't that what we should expect from ourselves? Not perfection, but just to try our best?

BEAN AND CHEESE QUESADILLAS

If you find yourself one evening thinking "I don't know what to make for dinner. I wonder what Carrie's making?" chances are I'll be making bean and cheese quesadillas. They tend to be my fallback meal when I'm out of time or can't think of anything else to make. What I love about them is that they're quick to make and I feel like my kids are getting a healthy dinner. I make them with the beans and cheese inside and then pile the rest of the fixings on top. And truth be told, I tend to use fresh pre-made salsa from my grocery store, as well as pre-shredded cheese from a bag. We're just doin' our best here, people!

10 flour or corn tortillas

1 15-oz. can black beans, drained and rinsed

Shredded cheese — Cheddar, Monterey Jack, etc.

Olive oil

Salsa

1 avocado, peeled and sliced

Sour cream

Heat a heavy-bottomed skillet (my favorite is my cast iron skillet) over medium heat. Sprinkle some beans and cheese evenly over one tortilla and top that with another tortilla. Brush the top tortilla with olive oil and carefully brush your skillet with olive oil. Lay your quesadilla in the pan and cook until nicely browned on one side, about 2 minutes. Flip and cook another 2 minutes or so. Take care that the tortillas do not brown too quickly. You may need to turn your heat down. Take the quesadilla out of the pan when the cheese is melted and both sides are nicely browned.

Cut each quesadilla into four triangles. Top each triangle with a couple slices of avocado, a scoop of salsa, and a dollop of sour cream. Enjoy!

YIELD: 5 quick quesadillas

GOING UNDERCOVER WITH ROASTED SQUASH SOUP

I'm not gonna lie. Squash tends to be more appreciated by the females in our house along with her sister foods: risotto, quiche, and salads containing nuts, avocados, and crumbled Gorgonzola.

The green stuff — broccoli, spinach, Brussels sprouts — I can get the males of this family to eat, but unless it's in a pumpkin pie, they scoff at the orange winter staple. And believe me, I have tried.

I've roasted it with butter. I've put it in pasta with broccoli rabe, pancetta, and pepitas. I've put it in a mild soup with apples, in a spicy soup with cayenne pepper, and in a minestrone soup with pasta. I have stopped short of topping it with loads of butter, brown sugar, and marshmallows because at that point, I think, "Let's just make s'mores."

Last fall, I attended a cooking class and watched as the instructor made roasted squash soup and served it to us in mini-pumpkins. I remember loving it…as well as the hot spiked drink she handed us as we arrived for the class. Each spoonful of soup was like lowering myself into a comfy chair and curling up with a book and a cup of tea.

Because of the fond memories, I recently decided to whip up my own roasted squash soup (minus the cute pumpkins) and try it out on my family.

My daughter grabbed a bowl, filled it up, and promptly devoured it like it was ice cream. My hubby filled up a bowl, covered the top with pancetta bits, and like a good boy, dutifully ate his dinner. The boys stabbed at it with their spoons as if it were porridge; they had apple slices and bread for dinner that night. I went back for seconds and ate it every day for lunch that week.

One of my favorite people to cook for is my father. He loves food. Not in an unhealthy, consume bag-after-bag-of-potato-chips kind of way, but in a way that shows his appreciation for how delicious something is and how much it means to him that someone made it for him. If he loves your meal, he will let you know and you will be filled with warm feelings from head to toe. He'll also let you know if he doesn't like it or if it needs more salt…so there's that.

My parents came over for soup and pumpkin carving a couple Sundays ago. I decided to do a secret little test on the whole family. Who would eat the squash soup? I made a pot of the roasted squash soup, set it next to a pot of my ham and white bean soup, and let the experiment play out.

All three of my males ate the ham and bean soup. My mom and my daughter had a bowl of each kind. I ate the squash soup and I had a tough time figuring out just what my dad ate.

Before my parents headed home, I mentioned to my mom that we had a little bit of squash soup left over and she was welcome to take some home with her. At that point, my Dad piped up proudly, "By the way, I mixed the squash soup together with the ham and bean soup. It was wuuunderful!"

"Interesting," I thought. Experiment completed.

I'm still on the hunt for a male-friendly squash recipe for Minns men, however, I highly recommend this soup for a book club dinner, wine night with the gals, or a girls' weekend away served with the aforementioned salad containing nuts, avocados, and crumbled Gorgonzola. Maybe next time I make it for my family, I'll put in the extra effort to serve it in the cute little pumpkins. I'll let you know how that goes.

ROASTED SQUASH SOUP

This velvety soup is a great choice for Meatless Monday, a night with the gals, or served to the guys in your life with a thick layer of pancetta bits on top. Take care not to slice your hand when you are quartering your squash. I use a large, very sharp knife, and cut through the squash using a seesaw motion.

1 acorn squash

1 butternut squash

1 tablespoon olive oil

Salt and pepper

2 tablespoons olive oil

1 medium yellow onion, peeled and diced

1 carrot, peeled and diced

1 celery stalk, diced

2 quarts chicken broth (or vegetable broth)

Optional: 1/2 cup white wine

1 teaspoon allspice

1 teaspoon dried sage or 1 tablespoon fresh chopped sage

Salt and pepper, to taste

1/2 cup half-and-half

Optional: 1/3 lb. diced pancetta + 1 teaspoon olive oil

Preheat your oven to 425°F. Carefully slice your squash into quarters. Scoop out the seeds and gooey strings. Brush meaty parts with olive oil. Sprinkle with salt and pepper. Place on a roasting pan, cut side up, and roast for 45-60 minutes or until squash is easily pricked with a fork. Set aside to cool a bit. Once cool enough to handle, remove flesh from skin. Discard the skin.

While your squash is roasting, prepare your other vegetables. In a large soup pot, sauté your onion, carrot, and celery in 2 tablespoons olive oil over medium heat until the veggies begin to soften, about 8-10 minutes. Add your squash, broth, wine, allspice, sage, salt, and pepper. Whisk to combine. Bring to a boil. Then reduce heat and let simmer for 20 minutes.

While soup is simmering, brown your pancetta in a teaspoon of olive oil for about 5-6 minutes. Drain on a paper towel and set aside.

When simmering is finished, remove soup from heat. Using an immersion blender (my preferred method) or a blender, carefully puree soup until smooth. Whisk in your half-and-half.

Scoop the velvety concoction into shallow soup bowls. Top with sprinkles of pancetta and a sage leaf for added loveliness. Enjoy.

YIELD: One big pot of soup

TRADITIONS TO KEEP AND OTHERS TO LET GO

Two days before Thanksgiving, I was standing in the checkout line of one of my favorite grocery stores thinking, "I sure hope no one sees me here." I was about halfway finished unloading my cart when I caught the eye of this darling woman smiling at me. She took a step forward and said, "Oh, it is you. Hi, I'm Michelle. I read your blog and I really enjoy it."

I smiled and replied, "Oh, hi…nice to meet you, too. You are so sweet to tell me that. Thank you."

As we talked, I tried to block her view of my conveyor belt with my body. She continued to tell me how a friend told her I like to shop at this store and how our daughters were at the same high school. Meanwhile, my mind raced to formulate a plausible explanation for why I was standing there with a huge tub of pre-cooked mashed potatoes in my hands. And why on the conveyor belt behind me there was also a pre-cooked turkey, stuffing, gravy, and Brussels sprouts.

I shared this story later with a physical therapist friend of mine. She laughed and said, "You being caught with an entire pre-cooked Thanksgiving dinner is like me being caught in a doughnut shop."

I came clean with Michelle. I came clean with my physical therapist friend.

And I'll come clean with you. I personally find that all of these holiday traditions that have been passed down to us over the course of generations are simply too much. We live in different times with different priorities than when the pilgrims landed at Plymouth Rock, or Ebenezer Scrooge was gifting geese, or Martha Stewart was (and still is) publishing photographs of her perfectly decorated holiday table and perfectly prepared food.

I don't want to spend all day in the kitchen on Thanksgiving…or Christmas… or Easter…or {insert holiday name here}. I want to sit on the couch drinking coffee in the morning talking endlessly with my brother and sister whom I don't get to see nearly enough. I want to play word games with my daughter even though she can beat me now. I want to listen, really listen, to my 7-year-old as he explains the drawings of a city he's created using what seems like an entire ream of copy paper. I want to cozy up with my 13-year-old and watch the Harry Potter movie marathon or hang out with my hubby, my mom, and my dad and watch holiday bowl games. And if there is time, I want to go for a walk…a long walk. What I've come to realize is I prefer to pick and choose the holiday traditions that I love best and let the rest go.

I love to make pie. For Thanksgiving, my contribution was four homemade pumpkin pies. We ate them for dinner and breakfast. I'm also a veggie pusher, so I added a simple green salad to our pre-cooked holiday buffet.

I love finding ways to remember the actual meaning of the holiday. Last year, I instigated a simple tree of thanks. Everyone who was here for Thanksgiving wrote down on a mailing tag a few words of thanks. The 7-year-old cousins took turns reading everyone's tags at dinner and the teenagers hung them from bare tree branches despite their silliness.

I'm thankful for all of the "mothers" in my life.

I am thankful for my buddy Carter, my best friend, Patricia, the time spent with family, and the Nissan 370Z.

I am thankful for Tow-mater, fire trucks, racecars, and milk.

The pre-cooked Thanksgiving meal was enjoyed by everyone just as much as the homemade ones of years past and the only stress I felt was wondering why there wasn't more for me to do.

I share this story because as we head into the next phase of the holiday season, I hope you'll be inspired to pick and choose your holiday traditions and let the rest go. Enjoy what you spend your time doing. And remind yourself over and over as you are letting go, "Martha has a staff. Martha has a staff. Martha has a staff."

SIMPLE GREEN SALAD OF FALL GOODNESS

I love making this salad around the holidays. It not only looks festive with the greens contrasting with the apples, but it also uses ingredients that celebrate fall right before we leave them behind for winter staples. The vinaigrette can be made up to a week in advance and stored in your refrigerator. You can also roast your nuts ahead of time and store them in an airtight container. And honestly, you can wash your greens a few days ahead, wrap them in paper towels, put them in a produce bag, and store them in your fridge. Right before it's time to eat, you'll have only a few quick steps to get this salad onto your holiday buffet.

FOR THE ROASTED NUTS

2 cups pecans

2 teaspoons grape seed oil or olive oil

1/2 teaspoon salt

1/4 teaspoon freshly ground pepper

FOR THE VINAIGRETTE

1/4 cup apple cider vinegar

2 tablespoons shallot, minced

1 teaspoon Dijon mustard

2 tablespoons pure maple syrup

1/2 teaspoon salt

1/8 teaspoon freshly ground black pepper

1/2 cup extra-virgin olive oil

FOR THE SALAD

1 large head green or red leaf lettuce, washed, dried, and torn into bite-sized pieces

2 generous handfuls baby arugula leaves

1 large Honeycrisp apple, cored and thinly sliced

1/2 cup blue cheese, crumbled

1/2 cup pecans, roasted and chopped

Start by roasting your pecans. Preheat your oven to 350°F. In a small bowl, coat your nuts with oil. Lay them on a baking sheet in a single layer. Sprinkle evenly with salt and pepper. Roast for 5 minutes. Pull them out of the oven. Stir them around and put them back in for another 4-5 minutes. Remove from oven and set aside to cool. Once cool, chop 1/4 cup of pecans for the salad. Store remaining nuts in a an airtight container. Alternatively, set the leftovers out for guests to enjoy at happy hour.

Combine your vinegar and shallots in a blender. Pulse a few times and then set aside to macerate (marinate) for at least 10 minutes. Add your mustard, maple syrup, salt, and pepper. Blend for 30 seconds or so. With your motor on low, slowly pour your olive oil into the blender through the little hole in the lid. Continue blending until oil has been fully incorporated into the vinegar. Dip a bit of lettuce down into your dressing to taste. Add a little more oil, vinegar, salt or pepper if needed for your liking.

Wash and dry your lettuce and arugula. Make sure leaves are dry before tossing with dressing.

Right before serving, put your prepared lettuce and arugula leaves into a big salad bowl. Arrange apples on top, then blue cheese crumbles, and finally, the chopped pecans (if someone has a nut allergy, serve nuts on the side in a separate little bowl).

Toss with half the vinaigrette. Taste a piece of dressed lettuce. Add more vinaigrette if needed. Enjoy!

YIELD: 6 salad servings or so

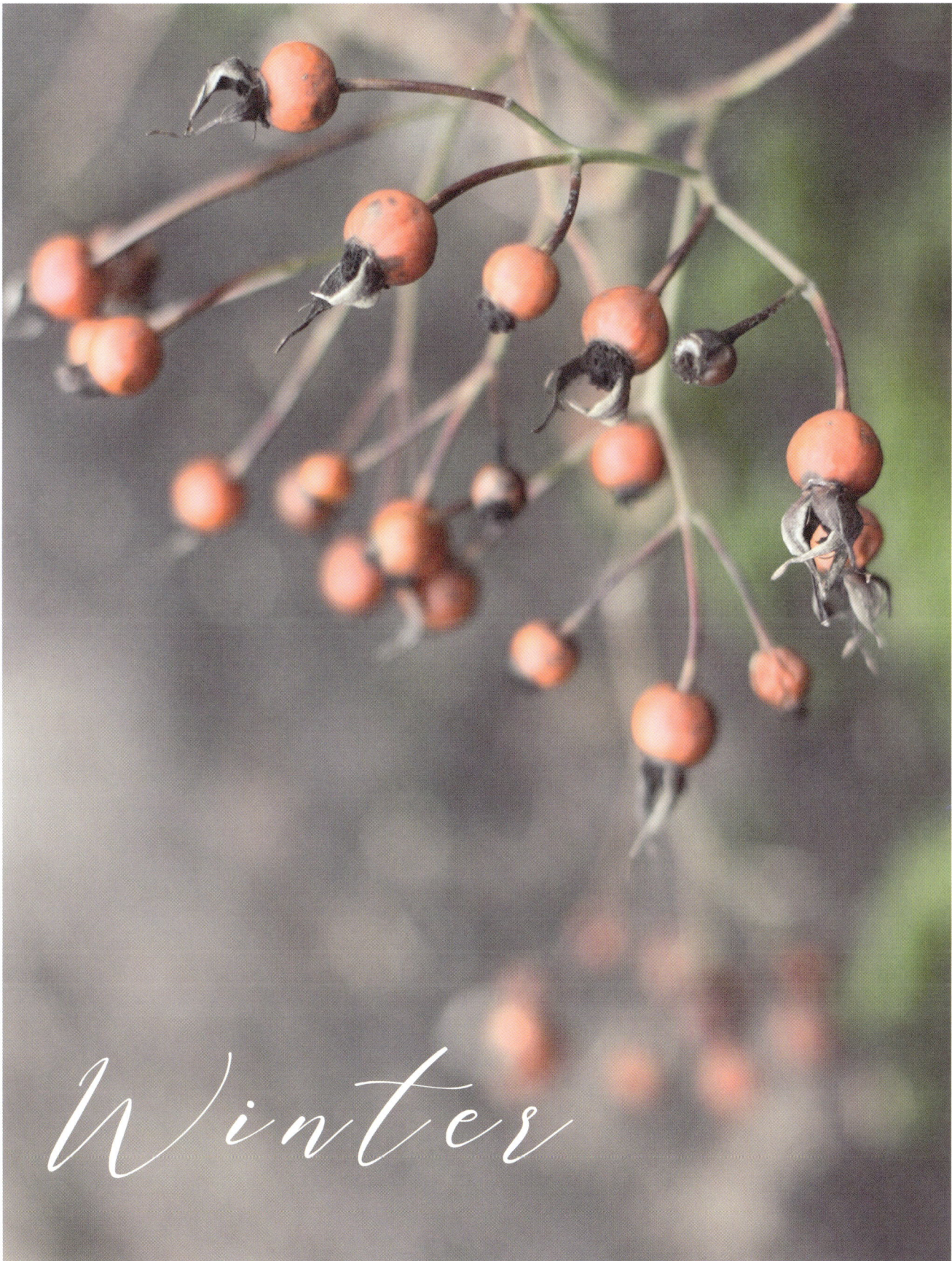

Winter

AN ELEGANT
SEPTUAGENARIAN CELEBRATION

As I sat at the piano, my back was on fire, my fingers were like dough, and my derrière felt as though I'd been perched on a cement curb for six hours waiting for the start of a parade. Furthermore, as I squinted at the music in front of me, I could no longer deny that I needed some form of optical assistance. What I could have whipped out with minimal practicing twenty years ago now required hours, days, even weeks at the piano; however, I did not breathe a word of my aches and pains to my main squeeze. I did not want the "You are a glutton for punishment" speech.

A few weeks earlier, I had agreed to play the piano at the 70th birthday party for a dear friend's mother. The party would feature a show tunes sing-along, soloists, women dressed in cocktail dresses from various decades, men in vintage tuxedos, gimlets, and Cole Porter songs playing in the background of a stately, 100-year-old Portland home. And at the center of it all: a grand piano.

I practiced for weeks. The evening of the party finally arrived. Greetings and laughter, air kisses and warm embraces, dim lights and sparkling rhinestones, clinking glasses and trays of hors d'oeuvres, coats being whisked up the staircase, and a table full of delectable finger foods all set a festive and elegant mood.

Partway through the evening, we gathered in the living room to roast the birthday girl, who wore a svelte black dress from the 60s with a Peter Pan collar of rhinestones and a gardenia tucked behind her ear. Friends and family from different decades of her life took the stage to regale us with stories about her, and as they followed one after the other, a theme took shape. This theme grew from the possibility that the birthday girl was lying about her age. She didn't look a day past 50. How could she be 70? Poems were recited and letters read all debating her age. At one point everyone joined in on an original rap song, which had us shouting over and over, "And she's still hot! And she's still hot! And she's still hot!" I started pining away for my 70th birthday party.

The soloists were up next. A few gimlets too many left the pillbox hat-wearing beauty wordless but she hummed "Smoke Gets in Your Eyes" beautifully. Soloist Number Two sang "My Funny Valentine" in a lovely, awe-inspiring vibrato. Then lyrics were passed out and the sing-along began. We sang one song after another: "Oklahoma," "Cabaret," "Wouldn't It Be Loverly," "Some Enchanted Evening," "I Dreamed A Dream," "Memory." And it wasn't just the women who sang. I clearly detected tenor and bass rounding out the four-part harmony. As I played with the voices surrounding the piano, the light dancing off the walls, and the genuine jubilation of the guests, I was honored to be included in this momentous occasion. The "back on fire" was worth it.

At some point, the lid to the piano keys went down, coats were passed out, and guests disappeared into the clear, cold night. Shivering, I hopped into my car. Driving toward home, I smiled as I planned my septuagenarian birthday party, secretly hoping people would chant "And she's still hot" at mine as well.

BLUE CHEESE AND WALNUT STUFFED MUSHROOMS

I'm always thrilled when I find stuffed mushrooms on a party table. They are like an entire meal in an elegant bite-sized package. In the past, I've shied away from making them at home because I assumed they were messy and time-consuming to put together — but not so. This recipe is incredibly easy and quick to make. If you're short on time, you can skip brushing the mushrooms with olive oil and sprinkling with salt and pepper. The challenging part is keeping the mushrooms warm once you've made them, however, people will pop these scrumptious little bites in their mouths, hot or cold.

24 medium white button or cremini mushrooms

2 tablespoons olive oil

Salt and pepper

2 tablespoons butter

1 cup leeks, diced, white and light green parts only

1/4 teaspoon salt

1/8 teaspoon black pepper

1/2 cup unseasoned panko bread crumbs

1/2 cup blue cheese crumbles

1/4 cup walnuts, roasted* and finely chopped

1/2 teaspoon dried thyme

Optional: fresh thyme for garnish

Preheat oven to 375°F. Line a baking sheet with parchment paper. Set aside.

Melt butter over medium heat in a small saucepan. Add leeks, 1/4 teaspoon salt, and 1/8 teaspoon pepper and sauté over medium low to low heat, stirring occasionally, for 5 to 6 minutes or until softened and golden. Remove from heat and allow to cool slightly before mixing with other ingredients.

Meanwhile, brush clean your mushrooms and remove caps. Save caps for a salad or sauté with eggs on the weekend. Brush your mushrooms with olive oil, sprinkle with salt and pepper, and place one inch apart on prepared baking sheet.

In a medium bowl, combine breadcrumbs, blue cheese, walnuts, and thyme. Stir in leek mixture until evenly distributed. Using a small teaspoon-sized spoon, generously fill each mushroom with the filling.

Slide your baking sheet into upper third of your oven, and cook mushrooms for 15-20 minutes, or until cheese is melted and bread crumbs are golden. Serve warm.

*To roast walnuts: Spread 1 cup walnuts evenly on a baking sheet. Roast in pre-heated 350°F oven for 10 minutes, stirring once halfway through roasting. Save leftover walnuts for salads or snacking.

YIELD: Approximately 24 stuffed mushrooms. Quantity varies based on mushroom size

THE BENEVOLENT JAR
BORN ON A BLUSTERY AFTERNOON

On a blustery Sunday afternoon, I dragged a heavy yard debris bag up our never-ending flight of stairs and questioned the decision to put my vegetable garden down — and I do mean DOWN — in the backyard. What kept me going, however, was knowing that my dear, sweet children were in the front yard dutifully raking the leaves. I was anticipating the relief I would feel once I saw the pristine lawn and garden beds made possible by their efforts.

As I mounted the last stair and peeked around the garage, I was met with silence. I stood there perplexed. Not a soul (or a rake) was in sight. "Huh. Where did they all go?"

I looked at the lawn. Better, but it still had a layer of leaves and the beds hadn't even been touched. With my load of yard debris still at my side, I could feel myself getting worked up. I heaved the bag over to the side of the garage and slammed it down. In long, heavy strides, I crossed to the front door, opened it up, and yelled, "Where are you guys?"

My eldest and my youngest immediately surfaced (already sporting slippers and warm sweaters), claiming, "We thought we were done."

The ten-year-old came out of his commando hiding spot about ten minutes later, grinning but clearly guilty. I, meanwhile, had grabbed a rake and started to forcefully rake up at least ten more piles of leaves. Stewing. Talking to myself. Saying things like, "Why do I have to be the only one to do these things? What kind of kids am I raising here?"

In that moment of frenetic leaf raking, the Benevolence Jar was born.

Later that evening at our family dinner, I presented the concept behind the Benevolence Jar. "Do you know what benevolence means? Anyone?"

Silence.

"I define benevolence as not just being kind but having the wisdom to know why you are being kind. Like last night, Daddy picked up dinner for us, served it, and did all the dishes to be kind, yes, but also, because he knew I was tired. When you say "Good morning" to your brothers and sister, you do it to be kind, yes, but also to show that you care about them."

I went on with more examples, and a speech about how a family needs to operate like a team with everyone pitching in. Unsure of what was to come, the kids remained silent. Then I laid two jars on the table: one filled halfway with pennies and one empty but labeled Benevolence.

"You three will need to work together to fill the Benevolence Jar. You do so by performing one or more of these acts of kindness that I've put here on this list."

I unrolled the single-spaced, three-page-long list that I had typed up after coming inside from the leaf frenzy. "I will tape this to the refrigerator for your reference. Each night at dinner we will go around the table and you will share the kind things you have done that day for other family members. You're on the honor system here since I can't be watching you at every moment. Should you behave selfishly or cruelly to members of this family, a penny will come out of the Benevolence Jar and you will need to earn it again. Once the jar is filled, I will treat you to a trip to the ice cream store, a round of bowling, or an afternoon movie. Your choice. We start tomorrow."

I could tell from the sparkle in their eyes that the game was on.

For the first week, pennies were going in the jar for clearing dishes, emptying lunch boxes without complaining, and remembering to say, "Good morning" or "How was your day?" to family members. The boys were the first ones to have pennies come out of the jar: one for teasing, one for biting. When the holidays rolled around, I packed up those jars and hauled them with us to the grandparents'.

As the days went by, I began to notice a difference in their behavior. Instead of pushing past his little brother to get to the sink first for hand washing, the ten-year-old consciously slowed down and let his brother go first. I found them asking more and more often, "Is there anything else I can do? Mom, can I clear your dishes?"

Of course, there were times when the whole process broke down, such as when my twelve-year-old daughter said to the teary, four-year-old, "Hey, I'm sorry I said chillax to you, dude, but you are waaay past grouchy."

To which my little guy yelled, "I just don't want to hear that!"

To which I commented, "Thank you for using your words to talk to your sister instead of biting her."

And my competitive ten-year-old, focused on filling the jar, perked up and said, "Can he put a penny in the jar?"

As we ate our dinner of butternut minestrone the evening before returning to school, there were six pennies left to put in the Benevolence Jar. At this point, the kids were pros and they ticked them right off with things like: Helping load and unload car. Waiting and allowing your sister to climb into the back of the car first instead of busting your way in and making her climb over you. Offering to take out the garbage.

The last penny went in for my littlest guy, "For not acting silly when talking to Santa about your list and remembering to tell him thank you when you were done."

When we were finished eating, the ten-year-old dumped the pennies out of the Benevolence Jar and back to their starting position. He then flipped a penny into the empty jar and skipped off toward the kitchen sink, hollering, "Cleared my dishes without complaining."

And so we began again.

As with anything, I'm sure the novelty will wear off, but I can enjoy it for now, can't I? And, perhaps, if I can get one last, job-well-done family rake project under my belt before winter sets in, it will all be worth it.

UPDATE: Years later, we still pull out the Benevolence Jars during the holidays. They aren't met with the same excitement as in the beginning. Quite honestly, they rarely fill up due to the lack of enthusiasm but they sit there on the kitchen table — their presence a wordless reminder to be kind to one another.

OH, YE BENEVOLENT
BUTTERNUT SQUASH MINESTRONE

As I'm sure you can relate, I returned home after a week of being gone during the holidays to rather bare cupboards. Not in the mood to head out to the grocery store, I decided to evaluate what I had on hand. The somewhat phallic butternut squash that had been sitting on the counter for weeks immediately cried out to me as if it were equipped with an alarm. And, so, I built this soup dish around him. Enjoy.

2 tablespoons olive oil

1 leek, white and light green parts, chopped

1 medium onion, chopped

1 1/2 cups carrots, about 3, peeled and diced

2 celery stalks, diced

1 1/2 cups butternut squash, peeled and diced (dice up and freeze your remaining squash for future recipes)

4 sprigs of thyme

2 tablespoons fresh sage, chopped

1 bay leaf

1 teaspoon salt

1/4 teaspoon black pepper

2 quarts chicken broth

2 medium white boiling potatoes, cubed

1 15-oz. can cannellini beans, drained and rinsed

1/2 cup orzo pasta

Freshly grated Parmesan cheese

Heat your olive oil in a large soup pot. Add your leek, onion, carrots and celery, and sauté about 10 minutes, until your onions are translucent. Add your butternut squash, thyme, sage, bay leaf, salt, pepper, and potatoes to the pot. Pour in your chicken stock, cover, and bring to a boil. With your lid askew, simmer for about 30-40 minutes or until your veggies are soft. Add the beans and the pasta. At a high simmer, cook for another 10 minutes, or until pasta is cooked through. If you plan to let your soup simmer on the stove for longer than 40 minutes, do not add your beans and pasta until closer to when you plan to serve your soup.

Ladle into shallow bowls and serve with the Parmesan cheese and salt and pepper. Add a basket of warm biscuits and some sliced apples or pears and dinner is served.

YIELD: A big pot full. Enough for a family of 5 with leftovers to pop into thermoses the next day for lunch away from home.

A REAL LABOR OF LOVE
FOR THE HOLIDAYS

A few years ago, Portland froze over in one of our annual ice storms. The highways morphed into long sheets of ice, but ignoring common sense and basic safety, I stepped into my car and carefully drove across town. The streets were deserted and an odd stillness to the city surrounded me as if my trek across town were suspicious. As if I shouldn't be out on the streets and why didn't I know that? But I had to get there. I had to get my plate of Christmas cookies. One year, the snow on the hill to my home prevented me from making the journey, but two days later, a plateful of Christmas cookies was hand-delivered. Last year, after a foot (or two) of snow was dumped on Portland leaving everyone stranded at home, my box of cookies arrived via the only group known to deliver through sleet and snow — the US Postal Service.

Every year without fail, one of my oldest and dearest friends — oldest as in, she's known me over half my life — spends 48 straight hours in the kitchen with her mother, baking batch after batch of Christmas cookies and candy. They bake ten, fifteen, twenty different kinds of cookies: chocolate fudge, almond shortbread, butterscotch bars, peanut butter with chocolate kisses, sugar cookies with sugar sprinkles, and my kids' favorite, Christmas holly cookies made with corn flakes and red hot cinnamon candies. When the baking marathon is finished, they invite their friends and family to bring a plate over and fill it up with their little "labors of love," as my mother would say.

This year, my daughter and I splashed our way across town. I enjoyed a cup of coffee and she a cup of cider. We taste-tested the holiday treats. We admired the Christmas tree. We chatted with my friend, her mother, and her darling, Christmas-sweater clad, century-old Granny. We filled our plate to the brim with treats and piled a second plate high with my favorite — the almond toffee. We hugged goodbye, hollered "Merry Christmas!" and dashed out to the car, just barely managing to keep our treats safe from the rain.

Hanna clutched the precious plate of goodies as we drove off for home. After a bit, she said to me, with a hint of amazement and genuine gratitude in her voice, "Mom, that was so, so generous of her."

I turned to her and replied, "That *was* generous, wasn't it?" We continued to ponder that act of generosity as we sped toward home where the boys were certain to be waiting for this year's plate of cookies.

CARRIE'S HOMEMADE ALMOND TOFFEE

When I was in high school, I insisted that everyone make and give homemade gifts during the holidays. My dad and brother labored over gifts made from wood and stained glass, my sister cross-stitched samplers she sewed into pillows, and my mom quilted bedcovers. I made almond toffee. I packaged up my homemade candy in little tins and proudly handed it out at Christmas time. I'm sure that when I outgrew the homemade gifts phase (undoubtedly to everyone's relief), people missed my almond toffee. At least my Auntie Barbie did. She told me so. Below is my recipe for almond toffee, which is quite similar to the almond toffee made by my dear friend. I prefer to use semisweet chocolate disks/wafers; however, if you cannot find any, you can substitute semisweet chocolate chips.

1 pound unsalted butter, high quality

2 cups granulated sugar

1/2 cup water

2 teaspoons vanilla

1 teaspoon salt

2 cups whole almonds, roasted* and chopped

1 1/2 cups semisweet chocolate disks/wafers, 66% cacao

1/2 cup sliced almonds, roasted*

Lightly grease a baking sheet with sides or line it with a silicone baking mat. Evenly spread your two cups of toasted whole almonds on the baking mat and set aside.

In a medium heavy-bottomed pot, combine your butter, sugar, water, vanilla, and salt over low to medium-low heat. Clip a candy thermometer to the side of your pot, taking care it doesn't touch the bottom. Cook your mixture, whisking constantly, until the ingredients emulsify (come together) and turn a caramel color. Continue whisking until your thermometer reads 300°F and/or the candy reaches the hard crack stage. You may have to turn your heat up a bit. This will take a good 15-20 minutes of stirring so make sure to let people know that you cannot be interrupted unless someone is actually dying. Your arm will get tired. Keep going. You don't want the sugar to rest on the heat or it will burn. Have an oven mitt close by. You may want to put it on if the heat from the pot becomes too hot for your arm. As you near the end, the mixture will puff up and become quite bubbly. Immediately remove the mixture from the heat when it reaches the appropriate temperature.

Carefully, so very very carefully, pour your candy mixture over the almonds. Using an offset spatula (one shaped like an L), evenly spread the mixture over your almonds. Let sit for 5 minutes.

Evenly sprinkle your chocolate disks/wafers over the warm toffee candy and let sit for a few minutes until chocolate is melted. Use your offset spatula to spread the melted chocolate out evenly over the candy. Sprinkle the sliced almonds evenly over the top of the chocolate.

Set aside for a couple hours in a cool spot away from direct sunlight to allow the chocolate to harden. When completely cooled, break or cut your almond toffee into pieces. Store in an airtight container. Best when eaten within 3 days or so.

*Roasting the almonds: Preheat oven to 350°F. Spread your almonds evenly on a baking sheet. Roast the sliced almonds for 5 minutes. Remove from oven. Roast the whole almonds for 10 minutes, stirring once halfway through roasting.

YIELD: A whole cookie sheet's worth of almond toffee broken into pieces

COMFORT AND CONVERSATION
FOUND IN A CUP OF TEA

I wish I could say that I spent my college years drinking coffee or tea in a sophisticated manner at some off-beat coffee house and reading the great works of literature cover to cover. But, no. I was the Diet Coke, Mountain Dew-guzzling Cliff Notes reader. The closest I came to regularly sipping hot beverages was the spiced apple cider my mother served us during the holidays.

Following those proverbial years of intellectual development, two dear friends and I donned backpacks and trekked across Europe. A highlight for me was the afternoon we spent in a little teahouse in London. We sat in ornate white metal chairs around a circular table covered by a red and white checked cloth. The room itself was an enclosed glass conservatory like something out of Mary Poppins and we felt rather upper-crust surveying our tea menu and preparing ourselves for the delight that was to come. As I perused the menu, I realized that the only beverage they served at this teahouse was, in fact, tea. This did not pose a problem for my much more cultured traveling companions who had indeed sipped coffee and tea throughout college. So they held my hand, ordered me some tea, and when it arrived, showed me how to add a little milk and a little honey.

These days, I am a bit of a tea fanatic. I'm never without a cup of it in my hand. I start out the morning with English breakfast tea complete with a splash of milk and a teardrop of honey. The afternoon finds me sipping an Earl Grey or Moroccan mint and by the time evening arrives, I've moved on to chamomile. There's something comforting to me about tea. Perhaps it's the scent. Perhaps it's the way the hot liquid warms me. Or perhaps it's that I often find myself curled up on my sun-faded couch with a book in one hand and a cup of tea in the other. Or curled up on one end of that same couch drinking tea and talking to a friend, a child, my hubby, or my mother. Just yesterday, I sat in my kitchen drinking tea with my father, reminiscing about a recent trip together, and paying no heed to the stack of dishes in the sink.

I want my children to learn to enjoy a hot beverage. I want to teach them at least one way to slow down and breathe. Whenever I ask, they always agree to a cup of tea. My daughter prefers the berry flavored teas, my middle one peppermint, and my littlest one — he wants Ovaltine "just warm, not hot." They don't often take more than one or two sips but they smell it, they wrap their hands around the warm cup, and they sit and talk with me.

This morning before sending them out the door into the frigid 20-degree air, I fixed them each a mug of hot chocolate and fed them a slice of Cinnamon Apple Crostata straight from the oven. Truth be told, I never make them anything warm for breakfast except instant oatmeal, but something compelled me to do it this morning. Maybe it was the cold temperature. Maybe the holiday spirit seized me. Or maybe it was the guilt I felt for not having put up a single Christmas decoration.

With the cinnamon apple scent swirling around us, I watched my children as they ate their novel breakfast, sipped their hot drink, and chatted. The whole scene was like something out of a Norman Rockwell painting. I almost shed a tear.

I turned around and continued making their lunches. My back had been turned for not more than a second when I heard my daughter say, "Oh, baby, don't do that. That's where big brother breaks his pencils when he's frustrated with his homework."

I looked over and saw my littlest one licking his spilled hot chocolate off the table like a cat. My ten-year-old then said in his most sinister, bad guy voice, "You ate lead. Now you're gonna DIE!"

I rebuffed that claim and said, "No, no, you're not going to die, but licking your hot chocolate off the table probably isn't a good idea. Come over here and get a paper towel."

And with that, the Norman Rockwell moment was over. But perhaps if I continue to provide these opportunities for them to take time to sit and be with one another, each successive moment will last just a little bit longer, until it becomes a regular part of their day. Maybe?

CINNAMON APPLE CROSTATA

Our grocery store is still brimming with cheery Honeycrisp apples but my children's love for them is starting to wane. Here at the tail end of apple season, they are turning their noses up at the plates of sliced apples I place before them, so in an effort to mix it up, I decided to make this little crostata number. I've been experimenting with whole wheat pastry flour and managed to get some in the crust. I tried it once using all whole wheat pastry flour and the crust didn't hold together very well, so until further notice, I recommend the half and half route. And if you're like me with nary a Christmas bobble in sight, which you probably aren't, but on the off chance that you are, make this crostata. Even if your house doesn't look like the holidays, it will smell like them.

FOR THE PASTRY

½ cup all-purpose flour

½ cup whole wheat pastry flour

1 teaspoon sugar

¼ teaspoon salt

¼ pound (1 stick) cold, unsalted butter, diced

1-2 tablespoons ice water

FOR THE FILLING

3 medium-large Honeycrisp apples, peeled, cored, and sliced (approximately 5 cups)

1/8 cup all-purpose flour

1 tablespoon sugar

½ teaspoon ground cinnamon

Pinch of nutmeg

¼ teaspoon salt

2 tablespoons cold, unsalted butter

Start by making your pastry. Place your flour, sugar, and salt in a large bowl, or the bowl of a food processor fitted with a steel blade. Whisk or pulse a few times to combine.

Using your fingers or a pastry cutter, quickly work the butter into your flour until it begins to look like cornmeal with a few pea-sized butter pieces sprinkled throughout. If using a food processor, pulse for about 10 seconds to get the same effect. Pour your water in a little bit at a time, working it into your dough just until the dough holds together. If using a food processor, slowly pour your water through the feed tube with the machine running just until dough holds together, but not for more than 30 seconds.

Turn the dough out onto a lightly floured surface and gently knead it until it all comes together in a ball. Slightly flatten the ball into a disk. Wrap in parchment paper, put in an airtight bag, and refrigerate for at least 30 minutes.

While your dough is chilling, preheat your oven to 350°F and line a baking sheet with parchment paper. Peel, core, and cut your apples into thin wedges. Set aside.

To make your filling, combine your flour, sugar, cinnamon, nutmeg, and salt in a large bowl. Using your fingers, rub your butter into the dry ingredients until the mixture is crumbly. Gently fold in your apple slices and mix just until they are evenly coated with the filling mixture.

Roll your dough out to an 11-inch circle on a lightly floured surface. Transfer it to your prepared baking sheet. Evenly cover your crostata dough with the apple slices, leaving a 1½ inch border. Gently fold the border over the apples to enclose the edges.

Bake the crostata for 40-50 minutes or until the crust is golden and the apples are tender. Allow to cool slightly. Serve warm or at room temperature. With tea, of course.

YIELD: 6-8 servings depending on how you slice it

IS IT WHAT'S ON THE TABLE OR
WHO'S IN THE CHAIRS?

While my hubby would prefer to remain anonymous on these here pages, I do feel that there's something you should know about him. He is a man who knows what he likes and once he's locked on to that — bottled iced tea flavor, vanilla ice cream brand, favorite holiday cookie — there is no deviating. Now, this is a good thing if you're me. He's locked on to me and I don't have to worry about him straying off. However, because of his strong likes and dislikes, preparing a meal for my guy can be rather challenging. Whenever his hunting and gathering takes him out of town, I immediately start thinking about all of the dishes I can prepare in his absence, especially those involving mushrooms since fungi have never made my sweetie's like list.

One night when he was gone last week, I spent the early evening chopping, slicing, simmering, and scooping. I called my kids to the table and laid in front of them bowls of tender halibut resting in a fragrant broth of mushrooms and leeks. I could barely contain my anticipation of enjoying this fine meal. I rattled off a long description of the food they were privileged to have before them, but although the presentation was beautiful and the children ate dutifully, somehow

it was anti-climatic. There we sat — just me and the three kids — eating. And then sure enough, the ten-year-old farted and it was all down hill from there. Somehow it seemed silly to have gone to the extra effort for my offspring when they would have been just as happy with chicken nuggets, mac 'n' cheese, and applesauce.

After dinner, I cleaned up the kitchen and then went upstairs to begin the bedtime routine. I glanced at the chair in Hanna's room and realized I would not lounge in it that evening while eavesdropping on my hubby and Will through the wall as they rehearsed "Up On the Rooftop" for the preschool holiday program. And with my hubby gone, I found the silence from the downstairs haunting. No SportsCenter blaring from the TV. No hollering from my hubby to the ten-year-old to "Get down here and check out this play." Once I had the boys in bed and was scooping up the trail of LEGOS® left by the elusive LEGO-pooping rabbit that apparently inhabits our house, I looked over at the couch expecting to see Hanna snuggled up next to her daddy watching their favorite show, but no, they weren't there.

So although I was able to eat my mushrooms that evening, which were quite tasty, the pleasure was lessened by the

absence of my main squeeze. It reminded me of the saying, "It's not what's on the table that matters but who's in the chairs." After this experience, I've learned there is some truth to that, but can't a gal enjoy a meal with mushrooms from time to time?

BRAISED HALIBUT WITH MUSHROOM AND LEEKS

For years, I didn't cook fish. I only ordered it in restaurants. The whole process intimidated me. Now, the older, wiser me can't be stopped. We eat a lot of fish. Don't be put off by the fancy title of this recipe. It is so quick to make that it is worthy of weeknight status, especially if you buy already sliced mushrooms. While the recipe calls for halibut, sometimes I can't stomach its price. Instead, I make this dish with petrale sole, Pacific snapper/rockfish, or Pacific cod.

2 tablespoons butter

2 tablespoons olive oil

1/2 pound white button mushrooms, thinly sliced, about 4 cups

2 large leeks, white and light-green parts only, thinly sliced, about 3 cups

1/2 teaspoon salt, plus more

1/8 teaspoon black pepper, plus more

4 cups chicken broth

1/2 cup dry white wine

5 skinless Pacific halibut fillets, about 4-oz. each

1 tablespoon fresh flat-leaf parsley, finely chopped

Melt the butter and heat the oil over medium heat in a deep, straight-sided sauté pan with a lid. Add the mushrooms, leeks, 1/2 teaspoon salt and 1/8 teaspoon pepper. Cook until softened, about 7 to 8 minutes, stirring occasionally. Add the broth and wine, bring to a boil, then lower heat and simmer 3-4 minutes.

Season both sides of your halibut with salt and pepper. Nestle the fish among the mushrooms and leeks in the sauté pan. Bring the broth back to a boil, cover tightly, and reduce the heat to low. Cook until the fish is just cooked through, about 7 minutes. If using a less meaty fish, check for doneness after 4 minutes.

Serve the fish in shallow bowls, surrounded by the mushrooms, leeks, and broth. Garnish with the chopped parsley. Enjoy.

YIELD: 5 servings

A LITTLE INSURANCE PLAN IN THE FORM OF CHOCOLATE CHIP COOKIES

For months now, at the request of family members, friends, strangers even, we have dutifully removed our shoes and assumed the "back-to-back" position, while these people eyeballed our heads. And then, these same people would shake their heads and declare, "Nope. Not yet."

And so it was, the second week of January, in the midst of making dinner on an already rushed school night, that my sweetie said, "Hey, wait a minute, you two. Stand back to back."

To which I replied, "I'm in the middle of making dinner."

"Oh, it'll just take a second. Come on."

Once again, I dutifully removed my shoes, turned my back, and stood there staring straight ahead as my husband eyeballed our heads. Then, with a big grin on his face, he straightened back up and said, "Well, it's official. She's taller than you."

I knew this day would arrive. At least, I knew hypothetically — all those years of playfully saying, "One day, you'll be bigger than Mommy" — but I don't think I really knew what it would be like when it was truth. When my 12-year-old daughter would literally have one up on me. It's a peculiar feeling to no longer have that physical stature over another person, especially one who is your child.

Perhaps it was because I was feeling a bit insecure about my new place in the line-up, or perhaps it wasn't insecurity so much as a bit of wistfulness about the fact that my daughter was growing up and there was no stopping it, but the following day I hauled down my mixer from the top shelf of my pantry and went to work.

While my kind and thoughtful mother kept a steady stream of snickerdoodle, oatmeal raisin, and chocolate chip cookies going my entire childhood, my children have never known that cookie parade. Homemade cookies would be a pleasant surprise for them, or more specifically, her. It wasn't bribery. I wasn't planning on buying her love, her respect, or her devotion to me with cookies. No, nothing like that. I was still her mother, after all. I still had the power to take away her beloved cell phone, iPod, or favorite pair of jeans, should the occasion present itself. It was just a little insurance plan.

When my daughter arrived home from school a day later, she twirled into the kitchen and said, "Mom, whatcha makin'?" I didn't respond, but upon seeing me dropping dough onto cookie sheets she exclaimed, "Oh, wow! Cookies!"

The next morning, bright and early, there I was again baking cookies. Hanna thumped down the stairs, entered the kitchen, and said, "Wow, Mom. More cookies…um, thanks."

I replied straight-faced, "Why don't you take some of these cookies to school and give them out to your friends? We'll never eat all of these."

And that was my way of adding extra insurance to my plan by hooking her friends.

On the way up to bed last night, my daughter snatched the last cookie. She hollered out to me as she climbed the stairs, "Mom, I can't stop eating these cookies. They are so good. Oh, and Mom, my friends devoured the cookies. They loved them." I tried to suppress my knowing smile upon hearing this. Ahh, my work here was done. Well, not done exactly, but put in motion.

No matter how "big" she gets, she'll keep coming home for more of these cookies. At least, that's the plan — my little insurance plan.

CHOCOLATE CHIP COOKIES
SPRINKLED WITH SEA SALT

One thing you should know about me is that even though I don't bake much, when I do bake chocolate chip cookies I require a specific dough-to-chocolate ratio, which is why my cookies call for 1 1/2 cups of chocolate chips instead of the standard 2 cups. If I'm going to the trouble of making a buttery, sugary, chocolaty concoction, I want to taste more than just chocolate. NOTE: It is preferable to allow this dough to sit 24-72 hours before baking.

1 1/2 cups all-purpose flour

1 cup bread flour

1 teaspoon baking soda

1/2 teaspoon baking powder

1 teaspoon kosher salt

1 cup unsalted butter, softened (2 sticks)

3/4 cup granulated sugar

3/4 cup light brown sugar, gently packed

2 eggs, room temperature

2 teaspoons pure vanilla extract

1 1/2 cups dark chocolate chips, such as Guittard 63% cacao

Freshly ground sea salt

In a medium bowl, whisk together your flours, baking soda, baking powder, and salt. Set aside. Bread flour gives the cookies a chewy texture and prevents them from spreading all over the pan and into each other.

In a large mixing bowl, cream butter and sugars together for about 3 minutes with mixer on medium speed. Add eggs, one at a time, completely incorporating each one into creamed butter and sugars before adding the next. Mix in vanilla.

With mixer on low, slowly add in your dry ingredients just until flour is combined with the butter and sugar mixture.

With a spoon, fold in chocolate chips. Wrap dough in parchment paper and place in a resealable plastic bag or an airtight container. Refrigerate for at least 24 hours and up to 72 hours. DO NOT skip this step. This is where the cooking chemistry between the gluten and the eggs works its magic.

Once your dough has rested the appropriate amount of time, preheat your oven to 350°F. Drop heaping tablespoon-size balls of dough an inch or so apart onto ungreased cookie sheets. Sprinkle the tops with a bit of sea salt. Bake for 14 -16 minutes, or until golden brown with the tiniest bit of "uncookedness" in the center. Pull from oven and let sit on sheet for a minute or two. Move cookies to a cooling rack and let rest until room temperature. Eat and enjoy.

YIELD: 2 1/2 dozen as long as grubby fingers have not been pinching off bits of the dough while it was resting

NOURISHED BY A SPICY PUMPKIN SOUP
AND SO MUCH MORE

Even though I was out of breath and my legs were quivering, I managed to brace myself against the wind. I had made it to the top of the Cape Kiwanda sand dune. Years ago we nicknamed the climb to the top "Eight minutes of hell," although with the sand packed down by the winter rains, it hadn't been as challenging of a climb as in the summer when the sand gives way at every step. I yanked up my hood and tightened the drawstrings. The wind was blowing so hard it was howling.

I steadied myself and peered over the edge of the sharp cliff of red rock that plunged to the ocean. Looking up, my gaze followed the beach northward toward Tierra del Mar. I took in the great expanse of sand and the waves crashing onto it — so forceful and unrelenting.

Carefully, I turned around to face the wind and where I had just been, the beach I had walked on and the dune I had climbed. The sun was not out that day, just low gray clouds and bits of rain. Off in the distance, growing smaller and smaller as they walked away from where I stood, I saw them — a small group of women. Women I had grown so fond of. I watched as they walked in groups of two and three. I watched as one splintered off and the others regrouped into four. Walk-

ing. Talking. Sharing. Pondering. I thought about how each of us, so different from one another, were brought together years ago by our shared love of books.

Every January, we gather for a weekend to plan our year of reading. We come loaded down with books, reviews, and notes. And while the books are the catalyst for our gathering, we really come for much more than that.

Besides books, we come bearing food — lots and lots of food. This year, we started our days with freshly baked chocolate chip scones, blueberry muffins, coffee cake, scrambled eggs, and even apple pie. Lunches were eaten out but the late afternoon found us scooping up a decadent crab and artichoke dip with fresh bread and sipping glasses of wine. For dinner we enjoyed a medley of homemade soups — white bean and ham, vegetable, chicken, spicy pumpkin — served with warm ciabatta bread and a salad of baby greens, nuts, dried cranberries, smoked salmon, goat cheese, and homemade vinaigrette. Later that evening, someone passed around a plate of warm chocolate chip cookies which we moaned over and debated whether or not they were the perfect chocolate chip cookie. Did they have the correct crunch-to-goo ratio?

Each year, while we eat, drink, read,

and walk, we also share stories about our families, our lives, and ourselves. This sharing of stories — of taking the time to listen and of being given the chance to be heard — nourishes us. It nourishes us differently from the food. This sharing allows us to go home feeling at peace and reinvigorated about our roles as mother, friend, daughter, and wife and as a singular, unique, and amazing person.

Whenever I return from one of our weekends, I find myself thinking warmly about what was said, what we laughed over, what we spoke earnestly about, and what brought tears. As I go on with my life, I carry around the bits of wisdom given freely to me by these women. And for that, I am a better person.

SPICY PUMPKIN SOUP

About a month ago, my friend Christine served me this spicy pumpkin soup. I could not stop thinking about it and told her I just had to have the recipe. She kindly fulfilled my request. This soup is savory and definitely spicy. To make a vegetarian version, swap out the chicken broth for vegetable broth. The beautiful thing about this soup is you probably have all of the ingredients hanging around in your pantry right now.

2 tablespoons olive oil

2 tablespoons butter

2 medium yellow onions, peeled and diced

2 teaspoons garlic, 3-4 cloves, minced

1/8-1/4 teaspoon crushed red pepper flakes

2 teaspoons curry powder

1/2 teaspoon ground coriander

1-3 pinches ground cayenne pepper

3 15-oz. cans pumpkin puree

6 cups chicken or vegetable broth

2 cups milk

Salt & pepper, to taste

Optional toppings: pepitas (toasted pumpkin seeds), sour cream or crème fraîche, bacon or pancetta, diced and cooked

In a large soup pot, melt/heat your butter and olive oil over medium heat. Turn the heat down to medium low/low, stir in your onions, and sauté them until soft and translucent, about 8-10 minutes, stirring occasionally.

Stir in your garlic, red pepper flakes, curry powder, coriander, and cayenne pepper. How much of the red pepper flakes and cayenne pepper you use depends on how spicy you want it to be.

Whisk in your canned pumpkin and chicken/vegetable broth. Bring soup to a boil and immediately reduce heat and simmer for 15 minutes. Whisk in milk and stir until heated through. Taste and add salt and pepper, if needed. Let cool a bit and then pull out your hand-held immersion blender and blend until smooth. Alternatively, you can leave it as is, or carefully puree the soup in a blender.

Ladle into bowls. Top with a dollop of sour cream or crème fraîche and a sprinkle of pepitas and bacon/pancetta crumbles. Serve with fresh bread for dipping. Enjoy.

YIELD: A large, soul-nourishing pot of soup

NOSTALGIC FOR THAT STRANGE GRASS SOUP

I have lived my entire life with different degrees of wanderlust. This is possibly due to being brought up in a military family. Or perhaps it's my own genetic tic since my sister doesn't seem to feel the same way: "I like the idea of it, but…" Me? Wherever I am, I find I want to be somewhere else. Not that the place I am isn't wonderful and lovely, it's just that there are so many wonderful and lovely places out there and I want to go see them. Experience them. Preferably as soon as possible.

Being a parent now, I can imagine how my mother felt while I incessantly begged her and pleaded with her to let me go and get on a plane bound for some far-flung destination. I'm sure it was with much trepidation and fear that she finally relented to allowing her first-born child, as a high school junior, to board a plane headed for Portugal to live with strangers for the entire summer. All without cell phones or computers. Just faith that it would work out and I would be safe.

Once my transatlantic plane touched down in Portugal, all of the other American exchange students and I were ushered off to a little school on the outskirts of Lisbon, the capital, where we stayed for a few days. The counselors spent that time trying to indoctrinate us into the Por-tuguese culture — food, language, kissing on both cheeks as a greeting — before we met up with strangers who would be our family for the summer.

For our final lunch before meeting our families, the organizers served us traditional Portuguese soups: a puréed carrot soup called Sopa de Cenoura and Caldo Verde, the national dish of Portugal, which I referred to in my journal as "that strange grass soup." Once lunch was over, they lined up all 25 of us on one side of the courtyard, and then they brought in our host families and lined them up on the other side. The counselors would call out the name of the exchange student and the families would run across the divide and embrace that person while the crowd cheered. It was all very exciting. In preparation for my trip, I had sent photos of myself to my host family and they had sent me photos of them so as I stood there fidgeting I had already spotted my host family and wondered if they had seen me as well. Finally the counselor called out "Carrie!" but before I could make a move this other Carrie came flying out of the line-up and ran to embrace my family. "But…wait…" I started to say, not knowing what to do in all the confusion.

Luckily, my host family had been studying my picture as well, and realized in a matter of minutes that this Carrie wasn't their Carrie. I stepped out of the line-up and gave a little wave as they were trying to rectify the situation. My host family and I embraced and I awkwardly exchanged kisses on both cheeks with my host parents and two host sisters. Then, they took my hand in theirs — they were big hand holders — and made me a part of their family for the summer.

For most of our dinners we ate salted cod with potatoes and garbanzo beans drizzled with olive oil. At huge outdoor family gatherings, we had whole barbecued sardines on grilled bread, Portuguese-style pizzas with thinly sliced chouriço or linguiça sausage, and tiny little snails, called caracóis, which were cooked with garlic and oregano and picked out of their shells with a pin. For our afternoon teatime, or *lanche* as my host family referred to it, we dined on moist, fruited, not-too-sweet Portuguese cakes. In return, I made my host family chocolate chip cookies and a carrot cake.

Recently, I decided to recreate a few of these beloved Portuguese dishes. After some research, I discovered that the grass soup, Caldo Verde, is usually made with kale and potatoes. Knowing that my own family would prefer a soup with a few more ingredients, I came up with a hearty version of Caldo Verde that still keeps some of its Portuguese essence.

The other evening, as Cesaria Evora played quietly in the background and I chopped up potatoes, kale, and garlic to make my soup, I thought about what it means to take someone into your home, to essentially have a stranger live with you, and to generously prepare food for her — your kind of food — and hope that she, this teenager from America, will like it. I have similar feelings as I prepare food for my own family each night. I hope that they'll like it, enjoy it, and maybe this food I prepare will hold some nostalgia for them much like the Portuguese food does for me.

A WINTER SOUP OF KALE,
KIELBASA, AND RED POTATO

People love this soup…well, except for vegetarians. It's a great recipe for feeding a crowd especially because it can be prepared a day or two in advance. I usually make it with turkey kielbasa but every once in a while, if I can find Portuguese linguiça, I use it instead. It's a bit spicier than the kielbasa. While the kielbasa comes fully cooked, the linguiça does not, so take that into consideration in your cooking time. Everything you need for a meal is in the soup, so I usually just serve it with some sliced bread.

3 tablespoons olive oil

1 large yellow onion, peeled and diced

3 large carrots, peeled and diced, about 1 cup

4 cloves garlic, peeled and minced

1 teaspoon salt

1 bay leaf

Pinch or two red pepper flakes

1 pound turkey kielbasa (or Portuguese linguiça), halved lengthwise, then thinly sliced into half moons

4 cups kale leaves, stems removed, and cut into strips

1 pound red potatoes, halved, then sliced into half moons, about 4 cups

2 quarts chicken stock

2 15-oz. cans small white beans, drained and rinsed

Grated Parmesan

Heat your olive oil in a large soup pot over medium heat. Add in your onions, carrots, salt, bay leaf, and red pepper flakes. Turn down the heat to medium-low, taking care not to burn the onions, and sauté, stirring occasionally, until the onions and carrots begin to soften, about 8-10 minutes. Add in your garlic and sauté one more minute. Turn your heat up to medium; add in your potatoes and kielbasa and sauté until lightly browned, about 8 minutes, stirring occasionally. Finally, stir in your kale and cook until it begins to wilt, about 3 minutes.

Carefully pour in your chicken stock. Bring the mixture to a boil, then reduce heat and simmer 45 minutes. Stir in your white beans and simmer another 15 minutes. Remove bay leaf. Ladle into shallow soup bowls and top with grated Parmesan if you'd like. Enjoy.

YIELD: Enough to feed a family of five plus leftovers for lunch the next day

WISHING YOU MOMENTS OF
CAPTURED TIME FOR THE NEW YEAR

Lately, I've been considering the evolution of holiday traditions: how they start, why we continue some and not others, how new traditions spring up and are adopted — Shelf Elf — or not. (I choose not.)

What occurred to me is that many of our traditions started out of scarcity. Feasts were held around holidays and celebrations because there was a scarcity of food. If you wanted a chicken or a fatted calf you actually had to raise that chick or calf, fatten it up, butcher it, roast it, carve it, and serve it.

There wasn't a grocery store nearby with shrink-wrapped boneless skinless chicken breasts or a pre-cooked Thanksgiving meal a phone call away. To treat your family and friends to a feast was a generous undertaking.

Gifts were given at the holidays because there was a scarcity of tangible, material things. Any of us who have read the *Little House on the Prairie* books knows the extent to which Mr. Edwards went to acquire and deliver Christmas gifts to Laura and Mary.

Online shopping with free two-day shipping or malls open from 6 a.m. until midnight did not exist. To actually give a person a gift, you usually had to hone your elfin toy-making skills and make it yourself.

And Hanukkah, well, that's an entire week's celebration focused on the scarcity of oil for a lamp.

All of this made me think more about what is scarce today. What can we give that would be a bit of a hardship? What kind of traditions can we build around that scarcity?

I'd say time. Time is scarce, precious, and finite. Ironically, it feels like we have less time these days, even though we have more timesaving devices available to us than ever before.

Maybe because of my focus on the scarcity of time, or tragedies unfolding around the globe, or challenges in my own life, I find myself frantically searching for bits of time I can capture with my family, friends, and neighbors. Small moments I can share with them this holiday season and beyond.

And so, even though there are times when I think that I'd rather continue checking things off my to-do list, I find myself paying attention when my littlest one wants to give me a dissertation-type explanation of his latest drawing of teeny tiny stick figures. I ride shotgun when my daughter offers to take me out for coffee again and again to practice her driving. I don't immediately say no when my 13-year-old suggests at 10 p.m. that we all pile onto the couch and watch a movie.

I spend an afternoon helping my mom decorate her home for Christmas and I carve out time to make and deliver edible gifts to my neighbors and friends. Afterwards, I'm grateful for the time I shared with them.

My to-do list will always be there. Time with those I love may not.

CHOCOLATE-DIPPED CINNAMON GRAHAM CRACKERS

One of my favorite grocery stores makes all sorts of chocolate-dipped graham crackers: chocolate and sea salt, chocolate and caramel, chocolate and peppermint bits. I have purchased and devoured these squares of bliss, but I have one tiny suggestion for them: use less chocolate. The chocolate to cookie ratio is off and I adhere to a very strict chocolate to cookie ratio (see my recipe for Chocolate Chip Cookies on page 185). In an effort to achieve a better ratio, I decided to make my own. These homemade graham crackers are such buttery, cinnamon-y goodness that they are scrumptious on their own, but the chocolate is a nice finishing touch. Make sure to use a butter knife or really shake your graham cracker after dipping to get the excess chocolate off, or instead of dipping into the chocolate, simply drizzle a bit on top of the cracker.

1 cup whole wheat flour	1/2 cup firmly packed light brown sugar
1 cup all-purpose flour	2 tablespoons honey
1 teaspoon ground cinnamon	Turbinado sugar for sprinkling
1 teaspoon baking soda	3/4-1 pound good quality dark chocolate disks, or bars cut into pieces, 60-70% cacao
1/2 teaspoon salt	
2/3 cup unsalted butter, at room temperature	Optional: sea salt for sprinkling

Whisk together your flours, cinnamon, baking soda, and salt in a bowl and set aside.

In a large bowl, mix together your butter, brown sugar, and honey until light and fluffy, about 5 minutes.

Reduce your mixer speed to low and slowly add your dry ingredients to the butter/sugar concoction. Mix just until combined.

Roll your dough up in some parchment paper or plastic wrap and stick in the refrigerator for 30 minutes or up to 2 days.

When ready to bake, preheat oven to 350°F. Line a baking sheet with parchment paper or a nonstick baking mat.

Roll out half of your dough on a lightly floured, clean work surface to a thickness of about ¼ inch. Using a cookie cutter with about a 3-inch diameter (star, heart, scalloped circles) cut out the graham crackers. Place them on your prepared cookie sheet about ½ inch apart. Sprinkle lightly with turbinado sugar to make them sparkle.

Bake for about 8-10 minutes, or until golden brown. Watch them carefully at the end. They go from golden brown (good) to dark brown (not so good) very quickly.

Transfer to a wire rack and let cool completely.

Continue rolling, cutting, and baking graham crackers until your dough runs out.

Once the graham crackers are baked and cooled, it's time for the finishing touch. Put half your chocolate in a microwave-safe bowl. I use a 4-cup glass measuring container because I like the chocolate to be deeper for dipping than it would be in a bowl. Melt the chocolate at 50% power, stirring every 20 to 30 seconds, until the chocolate is melted and smooth.

Dip ¼ to ½ of a graham cracker in the chocolate. Shake or use a butter knife to take off the excess, especially off the back. Melt more chocolate when the first batch runs out. Lay on parchment paper or a non-stick baking mat. Sprinkle the chocolate with a tiny bit of sea salt and allow it to harden completely. Continue until all the crackers have been dipped.

Bundle your homemade treats up in little bags tied with string and hand out to friends, family, neighbors — those you love. Enjoy.

YIELD: About 2½ dozen

MINESTRONE SOUP TO EVOKE MEMORIES LONG SINCE PAST

The tiniest of the three of us, Amy, had somehow managed to wedge herself in the back of the cherry red sports car for our drive south from the University of Oregon. Each one of us was feeling a bit homesick as the holidays approached, so our driver, Polly, was taking us home for the weekend — to her home. We talked while Polly's favorite holiday music, a Dolly Parton and Kenny Rogers tape, played quietly in the background. Since this was our first trip to Polly's childhood town, she had warned us about the hairpin turns along the two-lane highway. But she hadn't prepared us for the beauty of Smith River Canyon. Flashes of red, gold, and dark green zipped past our windows as we headed deeper and deeper into the forest, making our way to the northern California coast.

My college mode of transportation was a bike, and I was thrilled to have spent the five hour drive riding shotgun in the sports car. I felt only the tiniest twinge of guilt as Amy unfolded herself from the back of the two-seater car once we were parked in Polly's driveway. We entered her gracious home and for the rest of the weekend, we were treated to glimpses of her childhood and the bits and pieces that made her who she is: her bedroom with the canopy bed, the bathroom she shared with her two sisters, the plush white carpeting in the living room, the barn in her backyard, the motel her family owned, the bay by the ocean, her stylish mother, her father with the hearty laugh.

Sometimes I wonder if you can truly know a person without knowing her family, her hometown, and all the places and people that touched her during those impressionable years of childhood.

At dinnertime, we sat around the large wooden table in her family room, talking, and petting her dog. Her mother set down in front of us bowls of minestrone soup. The warm and comforting smell caused my stomach to growl and looking down into the bowl, I had to smile. Dancing around in my soup were black olives. The same black olives that we put on our fingers like puppets when I was little. The same black olives my grandmother set out at Thanksgiving along with celery topped with cream cheese and paprika. And suddenly, surrounded by my dear friend's family, in her childhood home, eating a simple meal of minestrone soup, I didn't feel so homesick anymore.

I find it funny how our memories work. Only the keenest among us can remember everything. Most of us only remember bits and pieces of fleeting moments. But no matter how many details fall off the edge of the memories from that weekend, I'll never forget the warmth. And it's those same feelings of warmth and family that define my dear friend to me.

BAKED MINESTRONE SOUP

Linda, Polly's mother, fed us the most fabulous minestrone soup. Here is my spin on that soup, which I make multiple times each fall and winter. I am not sure what the "baked" in the recipe title is meant to imply, but I am not one to argue with the original creator of such a scrumptious dish. Linda's instructions have you precooking your pasta in a separate pot before putting it in the soup, which helps prevent the pasta from getting soggy. I am always too lazy to do this step because it means washing another pot, so I throw my pasta in to cook with the rest of the soup about 15 minutes before I want to serve it. If you do follow Linda's advice to precook your pasta, add it to your soup just before serving. However you do it, I hope you'll make a batch of this soon and experience your own feelings of warmth and family as we approach the holidays.

1-3 tablespoons olive oil, divided

2 pounds beef stew meat, cubed

1 cup onion, peeled and diced

4 cloves garlic, minced

2 quarts beef broth

1 15-oz. can diced tomatoes, plus juice

1½ cup zucchini, diced

1 cup carrots, peeled and diced

1½ teaspoons Italian seasoning OR 1 teaspoon oregano, 1 teaspoon basil, and ½ teaspoon pepper

Water

1 15-oz. can kidney beans, plus juice

1 15-oz. can medium black olives, plus juice

1 cup shell pasta

Parmesan cheese, grated

Salt and pepper to taste

Generously salt and pepper your stew meat. Heat a tablespoon of olive oil in a large soup pot over medium-high heat. Add in half your stew meat and sear on one side, about 3-4 minutes, then toss and continue searing on the other side, about 3-4 minutes. The meat should develop a dark brown crust. Remove seared beef to a medium bowl, then repeat this process with the second half of your beef. Do not wipe out the brown bits that formed on the bottom of your pot from searing your beef. Those brown bits are full of luscious flavor that you want in your soup.

Once all meat is seared and removed from the pot, turn down your heat to medium-low, heat another tablespoon of olive oil, add in your onions and cook 8-10 minutes, or until the onions soften. Add your garlic to the pot and sauté another minute.

Return your seared meat and any accumulated juices to the pot. Add in your broth, tomatoes, zucchini, carrots, and spices. Bring to a boil, then reduce heat to your lowest low and simmer gently for an hour, partially covered. Add a cup or two of water if liquid evaporates down to where the meat and vegetables are no longer mostly submerged.

Add your kidney beans, black olives, and pasta and cook uncovered at a high simmer for another 15 minutes.

Taste and add salt and pepper if necessary.

Ladle into shallow soup bowls. Top with Parmesan cheese. Serve with crusty bread and Caesar salad on the side. Enjoy.

YIELD: One big pot full

SIMPLE YET REMEMBERED GINGER COOKIES

Last Saturday, I watched as my neighbor walked toward me through two-feet-deep snow while balancing a hot cup of tea in each hand. A few tense minutes later, she arrived at my front porch and handed me one of the cups. We sat down in my weathered Adirondack chairs and chatted. We watched our children build snowmen and engineer sledding jumps. We sipped our tea prepared the way my neighbor's Persian mother prepared it for her when she was a young girl — black tea with a pinch of cardamom and a smidge of milk. I've made my afternoon tea this way every day since.

The following day when my kids and the neighbor kids were inside our house warming up, my neighbor's six-year-old daughter tapped me on my hip and said, "Carrie, are we going to have those drinks again?" I must have looked puzzled so she continued. "Remember, the ones in the Santa cup? The ones with the sprinkles on top? Those drinks we had last year."

"Oh…the eggnog."

Every Christmas while I was growing up, my Granny served her grandchildren eggnog topped with nutmeg in small Santa cups. When the Santa cups showed their wear over the years, she doctored them up with red nail polish. Those cups were eventually passed down to me and I continue the tradition. Nothing fancy — eggnog bought from a store and a pinch of nutmeg, but always served in a Santa cup. Last year, I had set out a round of eggnog for the neighbor kids as they decorated cookies — such a simple thing, yet fondly remembered.

And then one morning this week, a dear friend and I sat on the couch in my quiet house. The winter sun was beaming through the window warming us. We each held a cup of peppermint tea. A plate of ginger cookies rested on the ottoman next to us. While we sipped our tea and nibbled on cookies, my dear friend talked — my friend who needed someone to listen. She remarked how those cookies reminded her of her childhood holidays. Somehow that pretty little plate of cookies took a sad moment and helped bring a little cheer.

Sometimes, when I find myself at the height of holiday madness embarking on yet another over-the-top project, I remind myself that often the most cherished bits of the holidays are the simplest.

GINGER COOKIES

My mom regularly made these cookies when I was growing up. I loved the extra sugar sprinkles on top and the way each bite seemed to melt in my mouth…well, actually, the "melting" might have occurred because I had a curious habit of sucking on each bite. This recipe originally called for using shortening but because I have a deep love for butter, I made some adjustments to the recipe to accommodate my love. These cookies have so much spicy goodness, I find they are best cooked and eaten bite-sized. I encourage you to make these if you have teenagers who have been spending too much time glued to a screen in some far-off place in your house. They won't be able to resist the smell and will eventually find their way to the kitchen, at which point you can try to engage them as you pass over a few cookies. Sometimes it works, sometimes it doesn't. Teenagers are funny little creatures.

2 1/4 cups all-purpose flour	*1/4 teaspoon salt*
2 teaspoons baking soda	*3/4 cup unsalted butter*
1/2 teaspoon cloves	*1 cup granulated sugar*
1/2 teaspoon cinnamon	*1 egg*
1/4 teaspoon ginger	*1/3 cup molasses*

Preheat oven to 350°F. In a medium bowl, whisk together your flour, baking soda, cloves, cinnamon, ginger, and salt. Set aside.

Using an electric mixer on medium speed, cream together your butter and sugar in a large mixing bowl for about 3 minutes. Add your egg and mix until completely incorporated with your butter and sugar. Stir in your molasses.

Reduce your speed to low, and slowly add in your dry ingredients just until combined.

Drop teaspoon-size balls of dough an inch apart onto ungreased baking sheets. Sprinkle the tops with a bit of extra sugar for sparkle. Bake for 10 minutes. Cookies will flatten and crackle on top. Pull from oven and let sit on sheet for a minute. Move cookies to a cooling rack. Eat warm. Eat cold. Enjoy!

YIELD: 2 dozen, give or take

FRAGRANT OATMEAL TO SAVOR
DURING THE QUIET MOMENTS

W ell, we're in the midst of it," you hear yourself say to yourself with a sigh: winter break, Christmas vacation, the holidays. And you want to be That Mom — the one who is fun all the time — really you do, but you have an aversion to noise. With each passing day that draws Christmas nearer, your children become that much more excitable and louder and you become that much more irritable and cranky. You can't really be angry with them, no, because they are truly giddy with glee and you want to feel their glee but all you feel is the pounding.

The pounding that is brought on by your sweet 13-year-old daughter, who for no apparent reason other than sheer joy starts running through the house, and at almost 5 feet 8 inches tall, that makes for some loud footsteps. Of course, her brothers who adore her every move (especially the 11-year-old) start following her, swinging over the furniture like chimpanzees, and then the five-year-old, who isn't quite as adept at the swinging as his older brother, gets stuck atop a chair and almost knocks over a gigantic snow globe as he tries to swing his leg around. (Never mind the fact that they are not even supposed to be climbing on the furniture.) It's at that instant that you feel the stress level in your body move up a notch.

But somehow you keep moving forward — stress and all — checking things off your list. You manage to get everyone into bed, after which you collapse into yours and fall sound asleep only to wake up at 5:30 a.m. thinking about what you need to get done that day.

You quietly slip out from under the covers and head downstairs. You flick on the lights of the Christmas tree; they sparkle against the windows and a still dark sky. You sit down at your worn kitchen table — the one that has stoically held up after years and years of craft projects — with your cup of tea. In the background, Silent Night is playing — your favorite Christmas carol. The carol you sing to your five-year-old every time you tuck him in. The one you used to sing to your older children until it was too awkward to tuck them in with a lullaby.

It's not long before you hear a door open and then the sound of LEGO® pieces clinking against each other. The five-year-old is up. You rise from your seat and head into the kitchen. As you stand at the counter slicing apples, you notice that the sky is starting to brighten. You gently sauté your fruit in butter, brown sugar, and cinnamon while oatmeal gurgles in a pot on the back of the stove. Your two eldest slip down the stairs. They both have those sleepy eyes; those eyes that no matter how old they get are the same ones that looked at you when they were sleepy babies.

You call them over to the table and set down in front of them bowls of oatmeal topped with the cinnamon apples and for just a moment, everyone is awake and everyone is calm.

And then the sugar from the apples hits their systems and it's back to swinging over the furniture, but you tell yourself you can persevere through the chaos because you know tomorrow morning, a little slice of calm will be waiting for you.

FRAGRANT OATMEAL WITH CINNAMON APPLES

I love oatmeal. It's probably my favorite breakfast dish. I'm always trying to find ways to entice the kids to eat the homemade version as opposed to the kind that comes in a little packet. They LOVED this. If you don't like your oatmeal milky, you can always substitute water for the milk. I prefer my oatmeal not too sugary but you can add more honey if you like yours fairly sweet. Also, you can substitute the apples with a good baking pear such as Bosc or Bartlett.

1 cup milk

1/2-1 cup water (less water equals a thicker oatmeal)

1 cup old fashioned rolled oats (NOT instant oats)

1 pinch kosher salt

1/2 teaspoon vanilla

1 teaspoon honey

2 tablespoons unsalted butter

2 baking apples, peeled, cored, and thinly sliced (Honeycrisp, Granny Smith, McIntosh, etc.)

2 tablespoons light brown sugar (lightly packed)

1/2 teaspoon ground cinnamon

1/8 teaspoon ground allspice

1/8 teaspoon ground cloves

Optional: toasted walnut pieces

In a medium saucepan over medium heat, bring your milk, water, and salt to a boil. Stir in your oats and vanilla. Reduce heat and let simmer on very low heat, stirring occasionally, 5-15 minutes depending on the consistency that you like your cereal. Once it's done cooking, stir in your honey, remove from heat, and set aside.

While the oats are cooking, melt your butter in a large non-stick pan. Add your apples, brown sugar, cinnamon, allspice, and cloves. Sauté stirring occasionally, until your apples are tender, about 5 minutes.

Spoon your oatmeal evenly into four bowls. Top with your cinnamon apples and sprinkle with walnuts, if desired. Enjoy.

YIELD: 4 small bowls of oatmeal or 2 large ones

A SIMPLE REQUEST THAT WAS
ANYTHING BUT TRIVIAL

As I surveyed the enormous pile of puzzle and game boxes with missing pieces that sat on our family room floor, my heartbeat began to quicken. Yet, even though the tasks felt overwhelming, I wanted to spend the three-day weekend that lay before me organizing and purging. My kids were growing up and it was time to pass along toys they no longer used.

While I was concentrating on assembling a puzzle (I can't donate a puzzle with missing parts, now can I?), my daughter flitted by and said, "So, I'm having two people spend the night Sunday and we're making cookies for our community service project."

I responded, "Yes, that's what we talked about."

"Okay," she said and then added, "Oh, and some of us are talking about going to a movie. I don't know, like, tomorrow or something."

"Oh, okay," I said while silently cursing the puzzle with its odd-shaped pieces.

A few hours later, I was beside myself with frustration. "Where is the lead pipe?" Combing through a bin of random toy parts, I searched for the missing game piece. Seemingly out of nowhere, my daughter appeared. She said, "Okay, so the 1:50 p.m. movie on Sunday works best but we might change it to Monday.

We thought cookies from four to six on Sunday would be good, but if the movie happens we'll do cookies on Monday. Oh, and Maddie is coming too."

To this last bit I popped my head up. "Wait a minute. I said two people. That's it."

"But, Mom, Maddie needs her community service too, and we were already talking about it at school and I forgot."

Overwhelmed with the number of details coming at me and around me, I sighed and said, "Fine…but that's it. And who's taking you to the movies?"

"Probably one of the other moms."

I was making progress and had different piles labeled: Ready to Donate, Missing Pieces, and Too Far Gone. While I was sorting, my daughter appeared yet again and said, "Okay, Mom, here's the final plan. Sophia, Maddie, Abby, and Kenzie are going to the movies with me. Dad is dropping us off. You can pick us up after you pick up Jack from the party. Then Kenzie, Maddie, and Sophia will be here at six for the sleepover. Katie will be coming at eight. We'll make cookies in the morning. Oh, but Sophia has to leave early so you can just take me, Kenzie, Maddie, and Katie to drop off the cookies later that afternoon."

I sat there stunned. All I could manage to do was look at her and say, "Wait… what?" Somehow I knew I was being

scammed but I couldn't quite put my finger on it.

The morning of the sleepover, I sat my daughter down and said, "Now, here's the deal. I said two people. Somehow it's now five people. These are the rules. Look in my eyes. Right here."

"I'm looking."

"I'm not okay with you girls staying awake until five in the morning. All lights and screens must be off by one a.m., which means if you want to watch a movie you need to start it before eleven p.m. No kitchen raids after midnight. I'm trusting you to be in charge of your friends."

And with that I started up the stairs. "Uh…Mom?" my daughter called up to me.

"What?"

"Well, I'm just asking you because they were asking me and I told them I would ask you but would it be okay if Ella came too?"

"No."

The evening progressed like any teenage slumber party would. They politely ate their chili at dinner. Said please and thank you. But once my hubby and I had retired to our bedroom, they raided the kitchen after midnight and ran around the house whispering and giggling. At four a.m., my hubby went downstairs to remind them that five hours of cookie baking lay ahead of them and it would be best if they got some sleep.

Bleary-eyed the next morning (or should I say a few hours later?), they reluctantly started making cookies. They mixed. They rolled. They baked. They sighed. They decorated. They packaged. Finally, I herded them into the car and we headed out to drop off their cookies. Exhausted, I thought, "Never again."

We entered the warm and quiet house that sat adjacent to the hospital. The girls presented their goods to the manager on site. She explained to them that the house was quiet now because the children were out getting their chemotherapy treatments. She showed them a bulletin board with photos of all the families currently living there. She said, "I bet you're wondering why we asked for the unbaked cookie dough as well as the finished cookies?" They nodded. "Because within an hour of arriving at the hospital the children take on the smell of the hospital. It's in their hair. Their clothes. Their skin. The smell of baking cookies helps mask that smell and makes this place feel more like a home for them. And of course, the cookies themselves are a nice treat."

I looked over at the girls. Their teenaged bravado had been replaced with genuine concern. Perhaps they were realizing that what had felt like a chore for them meant so much to someone else.

All of my anxiety about organizing old toys and teenage slumber parties suddenly seemed so trivial when compared to simply wanting the smell of freshly baked cookies to mask the smell of sickness. As I dropped each girl at her house, I knew I would absolutely do it all again just to fulfill that one request.

LIGHTEN UP CHILI

This is a chili recipe that I go back to time and time again. Everyone loves it. I used to make this with two pounds of ground beef, but because our family isn't eating as much beef as we used to, I decided to lighten it up using half ground turkey and half ground beef. I like it even better this way.

2 tablespoons olive oil

1 pound ground beef

1 pound ground white meat turkey

1 medium yellow onion, peeled and diced

1 cup celery, about 2-3 stalks , diced

1 green or red pepper, seeded and diced

4 cloves garlic, minced

1 tablespoon chili powder

2 teaspoons cumin

1 teaspoon salt

1/2 teaspoon black pepper

1-2 pinch(es) red pepper flakes, depending on how spicy you like it

1 28-oz. can diced tomatoes with juice

1 15-oz. can tomato sauce

1 15-oz. can kidney beans, drained

1 15-oz. can black beans, drained

Optional toppings: grated cheddar cheese, minced cilantro, chopped green onion, diced avocado, sliced black olives, hot sauce

In a large, heavy-bottomed pot, heat your olive oil. Add in your ground beef and turkey. Season with a couple pinches of salt and a pinch of black pepper. Brown over medium heat.

Add your onion, celery, and red pepper to the pot with the meat and sauté 5 minutes or so. Add your garlic, chili powder, cumin, salt, black pepper, and red pepper flakes. Stir to combine and sauté another minute or two. Stir in your tomatoes and tomato sauce.

Bring to a boil then reduce heat and simmer, partially covered, for one hour, stirring occasionally. Add your beans and simmer 30 minutes more. Taste and add additional salt and pepper if necessary. Ladle into bowls and top with grated cheese and/or other toppings listed above. Enjoy.

YIELD: One big pot full

FINDING COMFORT
IN COURAGE

I like fresh starts. A new year. A new calendar filled with white space.

Last year, I wrote out an entire document of goals — four single-spaced pages. It was too much. Unattainable. This year I'm keeping it simple. Instead of starting with a list of goals, I'm starting with a word: COURAGE.

Every time I write something and send it out publicly for people to read, I put a little bit of myself out there and that makes me vulnerable. Vulnerable to both approval and criticism. Like and dislike. Understanding and dismissal.

Every time I take a photograph and put it out there for people to look at, a little bit of me is in that photograph. Once again, that makes me vulnerable and that vulnerability can often be frightening.

There are many days when I doubt my abilities and think, "Why am I doing this? Who wants to read this? Who wants to look at this? Who cares what I have to say or show?" And yet, I continue because I love to write and share stories. Because I want to be a better photographer and create art from snapshots in time.

Being a parent can be downright scary, as well. Never sure if I am doing all I can to ensure my kids grow up to be competent and caring passengers on our little planet. Never sure if I am finding the right balance between independence and boundaries for them. Trying to stay true to what I believe is right despite feeling as if my children and the entire advertising/marketing/social media world are fighting against me. But I try to remain steadfast in my role as parent. Hoping my kids won't sense my insecurities. My fears.

My six-year-old still does not know how to swim. He's scared. He mentally breaks down when he stands on the stairs in the pool with hands above his head like a rocket, and he has to push off face down in the water. He has to learn how to swim. We spend our summers on the Pacific Ocean coast.

Group lessons weren't working. His peers moved up at the end of each session and my kid was still bobbing. I had visions of him at ten, bobbing, with a class of three-year-olds. In December, I signed him up for private lessons. During the first few lessons, he bobbed, learned to swim on his back, and jumped in.

At lesson three, his teacher told him she was going to teach him the most important move in swimming. "The one that can save your life. How to start out swimming on your stomach and flip to your back to conserve energy. "

I watched him there on the stairs, shifting quickly from one foot to another, goggles in place, hands above his head. Clearly scared. His teacher held his hands and guided him through the move the first few times, but once it was time for him to do it on his own, he barely got in the water before he clawed his way up to find her arm, the side of the pool, anything he could grab onto.

On the way to the fourth lesson, he cried. He didn't want to go. He told me he was scared. I went over all the reasons why he had to learn how to swim and told him that sometimes in life, we have to do things that are important, even if they are scary.

He started out the lesson swimming across the pool on his back, but soon it was time to work on the flip. As he stood on the stairs, I could hear him tell his teacher he was scared. She waited. Finally, he pushed off into the water but then grabbed her arm right away. She put him back on the stairs.

He pushed off again and this time he started the turn but grabbed her arm halfway through. They were out in the middle of the pool.

She gave him a little push back toward the stairs and off he went, face down in the water. After a few kicks, he flipped over on his back and continued kicking until his head gently bumped the side of the pool.

I cried.

His teacher looked up at me with amazement. She hugged my little guy and told him she was so proud of him. Will looked up in my direction with a poker face, goggles on, and simply gave me a thumbs-up. He did the flip four more times during that lesson.

Afterward, I hugged him tightly and told him that what he had done was the true definition of courage: doing something that is important even though you are scared.

Whether you are someone trying to develop a skill or a talent, whether you are a parent attempting to instill confidence in your child, or whether you are a child learning to swim, there are times it can all be a bit scary to try to do those things well. To put yourself out there. To set yourself up for possible failure or criticism.

My hope this year is that I continue to have the courage to put my writing, my photography, and my parenting out there because it's important to me. Even though there are times when I'm scared.

A COMFORTING RAGÙ ALLA BOLOGNESE
(A RICH MEATY PASTA SAUCE)

While I was typing out this story, I had my ragù alla bolognese simmering on the stove. The comforting smell of the tomatoes, onions, and meat was the perfect backdrop to dig deep and consider what I wanted from myself for the upcoming year. If you're looking for guidance in your life, I highly recommend making a pot of this ragù, then curling up in a quiet place in your home and writing out your thoughts.

What I love most about this recipe is that I usually have the ingredients in the pantry and the freezer so there's no special trip to the grocery store. Sometimes if I have mushrooms or a zucchini, I'll dice those up and throw them in at the same time as the onions and carrots. And while I love the flavor Italian sausage adds to this sauce, sometimes I don't have any on hand, so I'll just use the ground beef and decrease the tomatoes to one 28-ounce can and one 15-ounce can.

2 tablespoons olive oil	*2 28-oz. cans diced tomatoes*
1 medium onion, peeled and diced	*Fresh herbs: 3 tablespoons fresh oregano and 3 tablespoons fresh basil;* **OR** *Dried herbs: 1 tablespoon oregano and 1 tablespoon basil*
4 cloves garlic, peeled and minced	
3 carrots, peeled and diced, about 1 cup	
1 pound freshly ground beef	*Pinch red pepper flakes*
½ pound bulk Italian sausage (mild or spicy, your choice)	*Water*
1 teaspoon salt	*1 pound dried pasta: spaghetti, bow tie, or penne*
Freshly ground pepper to taste	*Grated Parmesan cheese*

Heat your olive oil in a large pot. Add your onions and carrots. Sauté on medium-low heat for about 5 minutes, until they begin to soften. Add your garlic. Sauté another minute.

Once your vegetables are soft, add your ground beef and sausage. Break up your meat with a wooden spoon. Add salt and black pepper and cook until the meat is browned, stirring occasionally.

Add in your tomatoes and herbs (fresh or dried). Stir to combine. Pour in enough water so that your veggies and meat are just covered. Bring to a boil and then turn the heat down to low and simmer, uncovered, at least 40 minutes or up to 3 hours on very, very low heat, stirring occasionally.

About 15 minutes out from when you're ready to serve your meal, boil up a pot of water, toss in your pasta and cook according to the directions on the package, usually about 10 minutes. Drain the pasta.

Spoon your sauce over your pasta, sprinkle some Parmesan cheese on top and enjoy. Or, if you can possibly stand it, wait and eat it the next day. (You may have to add a little water to it when reheating.) The flavors will have mellowed and created this smooth, rounded bite full of tomatoes and meat and carrots and herbs. Simply delicious. Enjoy!

YIELD: One big pot, enough for a family of five and leftovers the next day

AM-I-DOING-IT-RIGHT RIBOLLITA?

My sixth-grader is hard on himself. When I sit down to help him with his homework, the first thing out of his mouth is usually, "I don't know if I did it right."

A few evenings ago when I started to read aloud a rough-draft essay of his, he cried out, "Oh, stop reading. It's total crap." I reminded him that he had already accomplished the hardest part.

This morning before Jack left for school, he said to me, "Oh, by the way, Mom, my teacher really liked my rough draft. You were right about just getting something down on the paper being the hardest part."

A few days ago, I was talking on the phone to my younger brother. We chatted about his sweet 18-month-old baby — a mellow, smiley guy who rarely cries. My brother lamented that he wasn't sure whether he and his wife should be focused on the picky eating, the potty training, or moving him into a big boy bed. "I don't know what the right thing to do is, " he confessed.

I didn't have an answer for him, because I didn't know what he should focus on. There was no single right answer. (I question my own parenting multiple times a day.) But then I thought of the wonderful baby my brother was raising, and the answer was obvious. "Whatever you're doing, just keep on doing it. You're definitely doing something right."

I don't have a lot of patience for repeating myself when giving instructions to my kiddos, especially when it involves chores or behavior that is expected of them on a daily basis. Instead, I tend to hang signs with instructions and reminders written on them so I can simply point to one when my children's totally faked forgetfulness sets in. I don't know if this is the right way to handle things. Maybe I'm passing on my addiction to lists and spreadsheets instead of actually communicating instructions, however, my littlest one has taken to the signs and has started adding his own addendums to them.

For example, I hung a sign in the kids' bathroom that read, *Please do not drop or slam down the toilet lid. Set it down quietly. Thank you.* To which he added a sticky note that read, *Don't pee-pee on the ground. Love, Will.*

Prominently displayed on the kitchen table is our family's Kitchen Table Creed that addresses proper table manners, language, and behavior to be used at meal times as well as the respect and gratitude to be shown to the cook. Will typed up and added an addendum that read, *The badest behavior will not happen at the dinner table. Using the words stupid, idiot, jeezus, jeezus-crice, etc. will not be told at the dinner table.* Clearly, something is sinking in for him.

I find that cooking is also a series of decisions that we constantly second guess. Did I add too many onions? Is the meat cooked to the proper temperature? Does it need more salt? Do I have to soak the beans? Can't I just use canned?

I recently made Ribollita — a traditional Italian soup recipe for using up leftover vegetables and bread. The name translates into reboiled. Sometimes with these classic dishes, I worry about whether I'm making it the right way. Is this how it should taste? Is this what it should look like? I took a chance and made it for the first time for a group of women a few weeks ago. I also served two other soups I've made multiple times with positive reviews. I gathered together in my mind everything I knew about making soup and combining flavors. I consulted various recipes as well as a friend who makes ribollita often. Then armed with all of that knowledge, I set about making this soup.

When I put it out for the gals to enjoy I was smiling, but inside I was nervous. I had no idea if I'd made it the right way. What if they hated it?

Of the three soups I served to my friends, the Ribollita was their favorite.

I-THINK-I-DID-IT-RIGHT RIBOLLITA SOUP

This soup is a great way to incorporate kale into your repertoire as well as to use up leftover bread. And no, you don't have to use dried beans, you can use canned, but the dried beans are less mushy. And speaking of mushy, a few of my family members prefer to add the bread at the last minute so it isn't quite so soggy. Also, if you can't find fresh basil, you can use canned tomatoes with basil already in them.* Sometimes I've soaked the beans overnight and the next day I find I have no time to actually make the soup. I've then drained the beans, stored them in the refrigerator, and used them the following day with no problems.

1/2 pound dried white beans — cannellini, Great Northern (or 3 15-oz. cans white beans, drained and rinsed)

Kosher salt

1/4 cup olive oil

1/3 pound pancetta, diced

2 cups yellow onions, peeled and diced, about 2 onions

1 cup carrots, peeled and diced, about 3 carrots

1 cup celery, diced, about 3 stalks

6 cloves garlic, peeled and minced

1 teaspoon freshly ground black pepper

1/4 teaspoon crushed red pepper flakes

1 cup white wine (or red, whatever is open)

1 28-oz. can diced tomatoes

4 cups Lacinato kale leaves, coarsely chopped, stems removed and discarded

1/2 cup fresh basil, chopped (*see note above)

8 cups chicken stock

4 cups sourdough or Italian bread, cubed and crusts removed

1/2 cup Parmesan cheese, freshly grated

If using dried beans, put them in a large bowl and cover with cold water by one inch. Cover with a towel, put in the fridge, and let soak overnight. Drain and rinse when ready to use.

In a large soup pot, heat your olive oil. Stir in your onions and pancetta and sauté for about 8 minutes. Add in your carrots and celery. Sauté another 8 minutes. Add in your garlic, pepper, and red pepper flakes. Sauté one minute. Add in your wine. Let simmer and reduce for about 4 minutes or until the alcohol has evaporated. Add the tomatoes, kale, and basil and cook another 5-7 minutes over medium heat, stirring occasionally. Pour in your chicken stock and your drained beans. Bring to a boil. Reduce heat and simmer 40-45 minutes. Check the beans for doneness. You may need to simmer another 5-10 minutes. (If using canned beans, add them after the first 30 minutes of simmering and continue to simmer another 15 minutes or so.)

Taste and check your seasonings. You may need to add a bit more salt.

At about 35 minutes of total simmering, add in your bread cubes and let simmer the last 10 minutes which is the traditional way to make ribollita. Or, do like our family does and sprinkle the bread on top of the soup just before serving.

Spoon into bowls and top with Parmesan cheese. Enjoy.

YIELD: One big pot full

THANK YOU

During the making of this book much sleep was lost, many pounds were gained, copious amounts of coffee were consumed, hours upon hours of dish scrubbing were had, and the mantra "athletic wear is the new black" was adopted as if divine decree. But most of all, incredibly kind people cheered me on through the entire process, and for that I am incredibly grateful.

My hubby has been president of my fan club since before I published my first blog post years ago. He never fails to tell me things like "Best post ever!" (every single time) and "These photographs are framers!" (every single time). And he has never wavered in regularly giving me a "Great job, lady!" even when it seemed this book would never get started and then when it seemed this book would never end. To have that kind of support and generosity every day in my home from my hubby is life-changing. Thanks, buddy.

Like my hubby, my children have been a constant source of encouragement. They assumed the role of my project manager: "Um, Mom, shouldn't you be working on the book? Are you done with the book yet?" as well as official and willing taste testers. "Mom, I think this might need a bit more salt." "Wow, Mom, we just ate that whole apple pie-thingy. So good!" "You mean the one I still needed to photograph?" But most importantly, they have allowed me to share stories from their precious and fleeting childhood and for that I am deeply beholden. Thank you, Hanna, Jack, and Will.

I cannot recall a single day in my life that didn't include my sister, Courtney Cook, and while yes, technically, I am the older and wiser sibling, I have no doubt that I've learned more from my sister than she has from me. My sister gets stuff done. When she wanted to start a band and cut a CD — she did it. Write and publish a book — done. Start and run a successful graphic design business — check. I eventually finish projects, but I have a tendency to overthink every aspect of them. Courtney inspires me to pick up the pace — to quit thinking and just do. She kept me going with our morning check-in calls and her witty text messages. And on top of all of that, her incredible graphic design talent graces every page of this book. Thank you so much, Sistah.

Another amazing talent that enhances every page of this book is that of my friend and editor/copy editor, Meg DesCamp. Like Courtney, Meg also helped keep me on task, but more importantly, she dusted off and cleaned up my old essays and helped turn them into something much more eloquent and clearly written. She made sure I considered what the reader would need to know — "Details, woman, details! How much juice is half a lemon? A tablespoon?" Meg was incredibly flexible — as I've mentioned above, my projects always take longer than I originally anticipate. And during the times when I would falter in my confidence, Meg always came through with an encouraging word to keep me going. Thank you so much, Meg.

Back when blogs were relatively new phenomena and even further back before the Internet existed, a handful of people saw something more in me than I saw in myself and took the time to tell me just that. Many of their unsolicited words of encouragement were given to me decades ago, long before I ever acted upon them, and yet I have never forgotten what was said and have carried their gracious words around deep inside me ever since. These kind souls may not even remember that they said anything poignant but I remember. That is one of the main reasons I continue to write, and to photograph, and to create. With so much love and gratitude, thank you to April Paris, Kris Samer, Polly Endert, Mara Cogswell, Audrey Monroe, Julie Lee, Christine Bornstein, Jen Rits, Shelley Zoller, Kami Ehl, my cousin Michele Lacy, my Auntie Barbie Rice, Dottie Cook, my mother-in-law Joan Kelley, my sister-in-law Kathy Johnston, and my witty brother Tim Cook who never fails to make me laugh.

And then there are those of you who have been with me from the beginning of my blog (or close to it). From back when I first gathered up the courage to put my writing and photography out into the world. Some of you are my dearest friends, some of you I know only through the web, some of you live next door, and some of you live on the other end of the earth. You have hung in there all these years and have regularly encouraged me through emails, comments, text messages, handwritten notes, and hugs. Also, there are those of you who visit my website regularly, but who are quieter about it. I know you're there. I can feel your presence (and good ol' Google analytics lets me know someone stopped by). A huge thank you to all of you for your encouragement and for spending a bit of your precious time in my corner of the web.

And of course, a big thank you to my parents, Betty and Ray. They have given me numerous gifts and opportunities throughout my life, but my elementary school years spent in a single-story house out near West Beach on Whidbey Island, Washington is truly the greatest possible gift they could have given someone like me. I spent half my time head down in books taking on the life of Jo Marsh, Anne Shirley, Trixie Belden, or Nancy Drew while nestled in the pink insulation up in our attic. The other half of my time was spent sitting atop cliffs and staring out into the Puget Sound as if I were Queen of the Sea, or skipping down wooded trails flanked by ferns and pretending I lived in my own secret garden. I truly believe that all that time spent up in my head imagining is what fostered my love of being creative. Thank you so much, Mom and Dad. I can only hope my children's childhood has been just as magical.

To everyone, thank you!

With so much love and gratitude,

Carrie

RECIPE INDEX

RECIPE INDEX

RECIPE INDEX